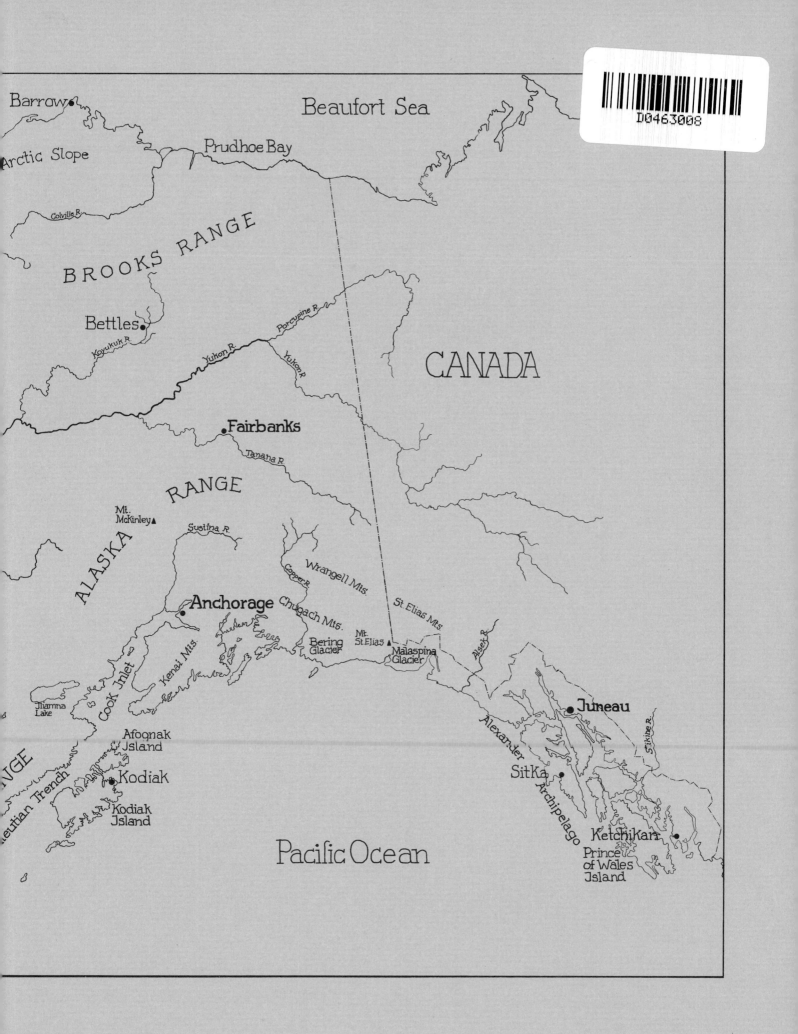

Barrow

Beaufort Sea

Arctic Slope

Prudhoe Bay

Colville R.

BROOKS RANGE

Bettles

Koyukuk R.

Porcupine R.

CANADA

Yukon R.

Yukon R.

Fairbanks

Tanana R.

RANGE

Mt. McKinley

Sustina R.

ALASKA

Wrangell Mts.

Copper R.

St. Elias Mts.

Anchorage

Chugach Mts.

Bering Glacier

Mt. St. Elias

Malaspina Glacier

Alsek R.

Cook Inlet

Kenai Mts.

Juneau

Iliamna Lake

Alexander

Sitka

Stikine R.

RANGE

Afognak Island

Archipelago

Aleutian Trench

Kodiak

Kodiak Island

Ketchikan

Pacific Ocean

Prince of Wales Island

Alaska
The Great Land

Alaska
The Great Land

Mike Miller and Peggy Wayburn

Preface and Epilogue by
Edgar Wayburn

Design by John Beyer

SIERRA CLUB   SAN FRANCISCO
1974

The quotations accompanying the photographs were selected by Peggy Wayburn.
Grateful acknowledgment is made to the following:
The Bancroft Library, University of California at Berkeley, for supplying the illustrations on pages 10 through 31.
American West Publishing Company, Palo Alto, California, for permission to reprint material from *Journeys to the Far North* by Olaus J. Murie, 1973.
Cambridge University Press, Great Britain, for permission to reprint material from *On Growth and Form* by D'Arcy Thompson, 1961.
Dodd, Mead and Co., New York, for permission to reprint material from *The Spell of the Yukon* by Robert Service, 1970.
Holt, Rinehart and Winston, Inc., New York, for permission to reprint material from *The Outermost House: A Year of Life on the Great Beach of Cape Cod*, by Henry Beston 1949.
Houghton Mifflin Co., Boston, for permission to reprint material from *The Pursuit of Wilderness* by Paul Brooks, 1971, and *Travels in Alaska* by John Muir, 1915.
Alfred A. Knopf, Inc., New York, for permission to reprint material from *Two in the Far North* by Margaret E. Murie, 1962.
Macmillan, Inc., New York, for permission to reprint material from *The Russian Expedition to America* by Sven Waxell, 1962.
George Marshall, for permission to reprint material from *Arctic Village* by Robert Marshall, 1933.
Mt. McKinley Natural History Association and the U. S. National Park Service, for permission to reprint material from *Mammals of Mt. McKinley National Park*, by Adolph Murie, 1962.
Oxford University Press, New York, for permission to reprint material from *A Sand County Almanac* by Aldo Leopold, 1949.
Random House, Inc., New York, for permission to reprint material from *Pelican in the Wilderness* by F. Fraser Darling, 1956.
Charles Scribner's Sons, Inc., New York, for permission to reprint material from *The Wilderness of the North Pacific Coast Islands* by Charles Sheldon, 1912.
Sierra Club, San Francisco, for permission to reprint material from *Glacier Bay, the Land and the Silence*, by David Bohn, 1967.
University of California Press, Berkeley, California, for permission to reprint material from *Alaska Wilderness* by Robert Marshall, 1970.
Walker and Co., New York, for permission to reprint material from *Nameless Valley, Shining Mountains*, by John Milton, 1970.

Printed and bound in Italy by Mondadori Editore, Verona.
Library of Congress Catalog Card Number: 74-78913
ISBN: 87156-110-7

Map art: page 106, 107, Gabriele von Rabenau; page 108, 109, Courtesy of the U. S. Department of the Interior, Bureau of Land Management; page 110, 111, Owen Welsh.

JAMES KOWALSKI

Contents

Photographs by: Ed Cooper
   Philip Hyde   P. B. Kaplan
   Bern Keating   G. C. Kelley
   James Kowalski   Wilbur Mills
   Olaf Soot   Bob and Ira Spring
   Tim Thompson   Bob Waldrop
   Edgar Wayburn   Peggy Wayburn

. . . to the great land, and all those who care for it

We gratefully acknowledge the generous help of the many
people, all Alaskans, who assisted in the preparation of this book.

Special acknowledgment is due to the Charlotte Mauk Fund of the Sierra Club
Foundation for its generous assistance to the publication of this book.

Preface

The rapid sequence of critical events in Alaska, beginning with statehood in 1958 and culminating in the discovery of tremendous reserves of oil in 1968 and the passage of the Alaskan Native Claims Settlement Act in 1971, has prompted the publication of this book. Alaska is unique among the states both in the vastness of its scenic riches and in the fragility of the interrelationships of land and life that have evolved in a harsh setting over millions of years. Decisions made in the next several years can alter the landscape and life of Alaska forever——with tragic and irreversible consequences.

Alaska is, as large format books published by Sierra Club in the past have been, a pictorial testament to the grandeur and beauty of an extraordinary complex of wilderness areas. Accompanying the photographs are two thoughtfully written views of Alaska. Mike Miller, an excellent journalist and one of Alaska's most able and environmentally sensitive state legislators, traces the fascinating history of his beloved state, and some of the inevitable problems accompanying its development since the first Russian explorers. Peggy Wayburn, a perceptive writer on ecological themes, has a special interest in Alaska. She discusses the rich variety of interconnected natural elements that make up this marvelous geographical entity we call Alaska. A final chapter examines the future of Alaska with respect to those lands within the state that, in the view of conservationists, should be permanently protected in the national interest.

But the clock is running . . . .Congress has given itself only until December 1978 to determine for all time how much of Alaska shall be preserved as National Interest Lands, as a legacy which we see as enriching all Alaskans, all Americans.

EDGAR WAYBURN
*Chairman Alaska Task Force,
and Past President Sierra Club*

1. Discovery and Development

MIKE MILLER

Among the volumes in Alaska's state historical library in Juneau is one that is neither history nor about Alaska. It is fiction, an eighteenth-century edition of Jonathan Swift's *Gulliver's Travels*, which was first published in 1726. Though a valuable collector's item, the book is in the library because of a map printed opposite the chapter entitled "Voyage to Brobdignag." The map shows Swift's fanciful kingdom as a large peninsula extending westward from the top of North America, a peninsula that bears a curious resemblance to the outline of Alaska. Swift's description of Brobdignag reinforces the comparison: "The kingdom is a peninsula terminated to the northeast by a ridge of mountains thirty miles high, which are altogether impassible by reason of the volcanoes upon the tops. . . . On the three other sides it is bounded by the ocean. . . . The large rivers are full of vessels and abound with excellent fish."

Alaska wasn't discovered by the Europeans until 1741. Although the similarity between Alaska and Swift's land of giants is mere coincidence, the inclusion of *Gulliver's Travels* in the state's historical library is not. Alaskans relish the comparison because they love to celebrate the great size of their state and glory in the awesome scale of its landscape. For that matter, so do people who are not residents of Alaska, whether they are conservationists, who delight in its vast wilderness, or industrialists, who are eager to develop its abundance of untapped resources. The "wide open spaces" that first beckoned Americans west now draw them, for various reasons, to Alaska. But size is deceptive. There is an attitude about the land of Alaska that was common a century ago in the Old West, namely, that the land and its resources are so vast that somehow they will last forever. History has already shown otherwise—in Texas, in Colorado, in California, in Florida, in every state. Alaska now offers Alaskans and other Americans a chance to discover whether they can learn from experience. The opportunities to start fresh still exist throughout Alaska, from the icy outposts on the Arctic Ocean to the lush forests of the southeast panhandle.

Alaska's abundance lured the first men to North America approximately 30,000 years ago, when Asia and Alaska were connected by the Bering Straits Land Bridge, exposed by the retreating sea. During most of the last Ice Age, the land bridge comprised a vast grassland that supported enormous numbers of grazing mammals. The first men in North America came here from Asia following the abundant game of an empty land. The ancestors of today's Eskimos and Aleuts were probably among the last to arrive before the land bridge was finally submerged by the rising seas at the close of the last Ice Age. Probably they lived much as they would for millennia and, to a lesser degree, they still do today: by harvesting the fish and mammals of the sea and the fruits and game of the coast. These last arrivals stayed on the Arctic rim, learning to thrive in the sometimes harsh, often cold, but always beautiful land.

Ten thousand years passed before the next men wandered east from Asia, this time across the open sea. In 1728, Vitus Bering, a Dane, was commissioned by Peter the Great to determine whether Asia and North America were connected. Bering sailed north from Siberia in a small, square-rigged ship.

Without seeing the coast of the New World, which lay obscured in fog, he decided that the two continents were separate and returned to Kamchatka only two months after his departure. He journeyed across Asia to St. Petersburg to present his report to the Royal Academy. The Academy was displeased at his apparent lack of thoroughness and ordered him to undertake a second voyage. It took Bering thirteen years to re-outfit, travel back across Siberia, and build two ships.

Two tiny square riggers, the *St. Peter* and the *St. Paul*, sailed east from Kamchatka in June 1741. Bering commanded the expedition and was master of the *St. Peter*. Alexei Chirikov, a younger officer, was captain of the *St. Paul*. Shortly after leaving Siberia, the two ships became permanently separated in thick fog and rain. On July 16, 1741, the men of the *St. Peter* finally saw the New World; the cloud cover along the coast suddenly parted, revealing the lofty St. Elias Range. Having sighted North America, Bering considered his mission accomplished and wanted to turn back at once, but his men persuaded him to put into a nearby island for water.

George Wilhelm Steller, a brilliant botanist, was assigned to Bering's ship to document the plant and animal life and describe the topography of the new land. His hopes for an opportunity to examine the flora and fauna were dashed by Captain Bering, who had little patience with Steller's mission. Rough weather was approaching, and the ship was running low on supplies. Bering's fears were justified, but his haste obviously frustrated Steller, who wrote: "The time here spent in investigation bears an arithmetical ratio to the time used in fitting out: ten years the preparation for this great undertaking lasted, and ten hours were devoted to the work itself." Bering grudgingly allowed the naturalist only as much time ashore (and on an island, not the mainland) as it took for parties in small boats to bring fresh water to the *St. Peter*. In the meager time allotted, Steller uncovered a number of Indian artifacts and collected several species of plants and birds, including the large blue-back jay that now bears his name.

Weeks later, a storm grounded and broke up the *St. Peter* on the rocky shores of an island just eight sailing days from the Siberian mainland. Here, Steller had an additional, if unwelcome opportunity to study North-Pacific-island life forms, while the rest of the crew, overcome with scurvy and fatigue, struggled miserably to stay alive through a long frigid winter. Steller himself escaped scurvy by eating native plants. He helped his afflicted shipmates by persuading them to do so as well. Before winter ended, Bering died of the same scurvy, exposure, and exhaustion that would also claim more than thirty of his men. The forty-six who finally escaped survived on a diet of island plants and

Walrus head. From *Alaska:* Sheldon Jackson (1880).

marine animals, such as the sea otter, sea lion, and sea cow. (Steller was the only professional naturalist ever to see and study the sea cow, a huge docile relative of the manatee. The sea cow was exterminated by hunters before the next naturalist arrived in Alaska some hundred years later.) The following spring, the remaining crew reconstructed the *St. Peter* from the wreckage and managed to reach Siberia, limping into Avacha Bay on the Kamchatka Peninsula on August 27, 1742.

The *St. Paul* had returned October 10 of the previous year, also having found North America. Her crew was as scurvy-ridden, filthy, emaciated, and depleted in numbers as the *St. Peter's*. The crew of the *St. Paul* had suffered one additional calamity. On July 17, shortly after having sighted the American continent, ten seamen were sent ashore in the *St. Paul's* longboat for fresh water. They never returned. The six crewmen sent to look for them also disappeared. What befell these seamen was never learned, but an incident that occurred a day after the second boat had departed suggested a grim answer. Two Indian craft were seen coming out from the land.

"These were American boats and they were filled with savages," wrote Lieutenant Sven Waxel, first mate of the *St. Peter*, in his account of the two vessels' expeditions. "They approached to within three cable lengths of the ship, then, seeing so many on deck, they turned back towards the island. Those on board the ship had now no boat left in which they could have put out after the Americans, and they had just to draw the melancholy conclusion that both the long boat and the jolly-boat were lost along with their entire crews."

Chirikov's men had encountered the Tlingits of southeastern Alaska, a proud, independent people who, for the next hundred years, would persistently resist the Russians. The Tlingits would ultimately have to submit to the presence of aliens in their land, but their immediate fate was far better than that of the Aleut (á-lee-oot, not a-loot) peoples, whose island homes were the first steppingstones on the Russian route east. The Aleuts were enslaved and murdered. When they retaliated, they were repressed with a brutality that was rarely equalled in the Indian wars of

Sea otter. From *Voyage to the Pacific Ocean:* Cap't James Cook (1784).

11

the Old West. Fortunately for the Eskimos and the Athabascan Indians, the Russians had no interest in the frigid lands to the north or in the interior of Alaska.

To the Russians who followed Bering, the new land promised a fortune in furs. Despite the hardships, disease, and death that plagued Bering's expedition, the surviving crew members returned to Siberia with a king's ransom in pelts, mostly those of the sea otter, which then numbered in the hundreds of thousands along the Alaskan coast. This lucrative bounty triggered Alaska's first era of exploitation. The worst of the Russians to follow Bering were the *Promyshlenniki*, plundering, murderous freebooters who in the previous century had slaughtered fur-bearing animals across the steppes of Asia to the eastern limits of Siberia. Until word of Bering's discovery reached them, the *Promyshlenniki* had exhausted new lands to pillage. Hearing of the lush new fur-breeding grounds to the east, they sailed to the Aleutian Islands.

The history of the *Promyshlenniki* era is well documented; the savagery with which these people subdued the Aleuts embarrassed the more civilized of the Russians who followed. Whole Aleut villages were enslaved, the women and children held for ransom, while the men were forced to pay tribute to the Russians. Many had to serve as hunters for their conquerors, leading them to the great herds of sea mammals, which were then ruthlessly slaughtered in enormous numbers. Treatment of the Aleut peoples probably improved with the coming of the Russian-American Company, which received an exclusive charter from the Tsar to engage in hunting and trading activities in North America. In 1784 the company established the first permanent Russian settlement in Alaska at Three Saints Bay on Kodiak Island. With the imperial charter came the imperial religion, the Orthodox church, whose priests made efforts to Christianize the Aleuts and provide some schooling for their children. Though scarcely something the Aleuts would have wished for themselves, at least they were no longer subjected to the extreme cruelty and exploitation that had been their lot under the *Promyshlenniki*.

Though the condition of the Aleuts improved with the coming of the Russian-American Company, that of the sea otter and other furbearers of the North Pacific grew steadily worse. By the thousands, and then the tens of thousands, the playful, unwary mammals were systematically slaughtered. At the height of the Russian era, after the indefatigable Alexander Baranov arrived to manage the affairs of the Russian-American Company, hunting parties containing as many as 500 or 600 kayaks would make summer journeys of hundreds of miles through the islands. Such fleets sometimes extended seaward from the large islands for miles, advancing methodically in small groups, closing in on any otter that had the bad fortune to raise its head above water for breath.

By the last decade of the eighteenth century, the Aleutians and the more northerly islands no longer yielded sufficient sea-otter pelts to satisfy the insatiable demand of the fur traders. In 1792, therefore, Baranov established a new settlement near the present site of Sitka. Two years later, the inhospitable Tlingits completely destroyed this settlement, but in its place arose New Archangel, which became the headquarters for the company and for Russian authority in Alaska.

Baranov lasted in Russian-America for 25 years, dying en route home to Russia in 1818. After his departure, the Russian position in the New

World began to slowly decline. Succeeding general managers of the company lacked Baranov's drive, organizational brilliance, and sheer guts. More important, the ceaseless slaughter of the otter and other sea mammals had all but annihilated the once "limitless" herds and thus rendered the enterprise unprofitable. With the decline of the lucrative fur trade, Russia's interest in Alaska waned. The Russians had come not to settle, but to exploit (a pattern that would become a familiar one in Alaskan history), and having done so, they were quick to leave.

At this time, Russia was fighting Great Britain in the Crimea, so fearing British expansion into a vulnerable outpost near Russia's eastern border, agreed to sell Russian-America to the United States for $7.2 million. On October 18, 1867, a day celebrated each year in the forty-ninth state as "Alaska Day," Russian-America became a territory of the United States.

It would be nice to be able to say that "Alaska Day" marked the beginning of an era of enlightened concern for the native peoples and natural resources of the Great Land, but what followed was, in the words of Alaska's former governor and senator, Ernest Gruening, an "era of total neglect." Not until 1884 did Congress pass the miserly organic act that formally established Alaska as a civil district. Though the lawmakers did set up a government, they did not appropriate enough money to carry out even the limited provisions of the act. Of course, the few Americans living in Alaska protested. Governor Alfred P. Swineford asked: How could he inspect and report upon the fur-seal hunting grounds on the Pribilof Islands, as the act required, if he had no transportation to visit the islands? How could schools be established on a niggardly appropriation of $25,000 for an area more than one-fifth the size of the rest of the United States? Such questions went unanswered.

In the following decades, when Americans did show interest in Alaska, they too often followed the Russian example: "Get in, get it, and get out." Nor was the federal government a much better steward of the land and its resources than Russia had been. For example, under United States jurisdiction, fur seals were slaughtered on the shores of the Pribilofs, and at sea, at a rate that made their extinction seem inevitable. Only an eleventh-hour international treaty in 1911 saved the dwindling herd. Convinced that Alaska was worthless real estate, the politicians and bureaucrats in Washington were not inclined to spend either time or money on "Walrussia" or "Seward's Icebox," as it was popularly known. Nor was the general public interested in or informed about Alaska. Few people could have named a single town in Alaska until the day in July 1897 when the steamer *Portland* churned into Seattle from St. Michael's, Alaska, with a contingent of prospectors who had brought more than two tons of gold ore from Dawson, in the Canadian Klondike.

Overnight the name of this unknown Canadian outpost was on everybody's lips, along with those of the Alaskan coastal settlements that would serve as its gateway—Skagway, Dyea, and Valdez. The last of the great Gold rushes was underway. Sixty thousand men crammed aboard rustbucket vessels from Seattle, Vancouver, San Francisco, and other West Coast ports to sail north. None of the routes to the Klondike were easy, and many men died attempting to get there. The best and most popular routes were Chilkoot Pass out of Dyea and the nearby White Pass from Skagway. The boat trip to western Alaska and from there up the

Kyackers. From *Voyage to the Pacific Ocean:* Cap't James Cook (1784).

Yukon River to Dawson was safer, but much longer. Other routes—across the immense Malaspina Glacier or west from Edmonton, Alberta, for example—were sheer suicide. Forty thousand prospectors finally made it to Dawson only to discover that the best claims had already been staked out at the time of the first strike.

Most of the Klondikers turned around and went home, but some, completely stricken by gold fever, continued their quests in the half dozen new stampedes that followed the big one of 1898. Most of these new strikes were in Alaska rather than in the Yukon and ushered in an era of mineral exploitation that has continued to this day. But the frenzy of the first gold rush was over. The business of gold mining changed from the excitement of discovery to the day-to-day hard work and routine of wage-paying production. Alaska once more dropped from the nation's spotlight, though it eventually began to receive more attention from the politicians in Washington. Slowly the population of the territory grew as prospectors continued to comb the hills and mountains looking for the big strike. Occasionally their skill, persistence, or luck would pay off, and where they found minerals in sufficient quantity to justify the construction of processing facilities, new towns sprang up—Nome, Iditarod, Fairbanks.

Even during the Gold Rush, some men came to Alaska for other reasons. Peter Buschmann arrived in 1898, not to strike it rich in the Klondike, but to harvest the treasure of the sea. He established the city of Petersburg on a small island along Alaska's southwest coast and built a saltery to preserve his catch. Petersburg has quietly prospered to this day: its population still catches and processes the salmon, halibut, and herring that first attracted Peter Buschmann to Alaska.

Peter Buschmann, however, was a latecomer. The first two canneries in Alaska were established in 1878. By 1889 the territory was packing more cases of salmon than Washington, Oregon, and California combined. By the turn of the century Alaska led the world in salmon production, and fishing had become its largest industry. The total pack of Alaskan salmon increased steadily through the early decades of the twentieth century. However, this constant increase decimated the fish population. At its peak, in 1936, the industry packed 8.5 million cases of fish, but by 1959, the last year of federal jurisdiction over the fishery, the pack had dropped to a mere 1.6 million cases.

From the start, a combination of industry avarice, federal apathy or collusion, and a mistaken belief that the territory's bountiful fisheries were limitless led the industry to do almost everything wrong for conserving the resource. Prior to statehood, Alaska had no control over its fishing industry, which was owned and controlled by outside interests operating out of Seattle and San Francisco. Not only was the industry owned and controlled by outsiders, it was largely manned by them as well, for the companies routinely preferred non-residents over resident Alaskans in hiring for the canneries or the boats.

The fish trap, an insidious device that was largely responsible for the rapid decline of Alaska's salmon population, became for Alaskans a symbol not only of what they hated in the fishing industry, but of their total inability to exert even the slightest control over their own affairs. The fish trap consisted of a fine wire fence, which extended offshore across major salmon spawning routes, and a large, enclosed holding cage, which each fish entered as it tried to make its way around the fence. During the processing season brailing vessels would regularly visit each trap, load the catch, and rush back to the canneries. All Alaskans, even those located in the interior, detested the fish traps, but could do nothing to persuade the United States Fish and Wildlife Service, which officially sanctioned the traps, to abolish or even seriously alter fish-trap practices. By allowing virtually none of the catch to escape, fish traps were rapidly destroying the salmon resource. When Alaska became a state, the fish traps were quickly outlawed. Before statehood was granted, however, Alaska endured one more era of discovery, this time by the American military. Six months after the Japanese bombed Pearl Harbor, the Asians invaded the Aleutians, occupying Attu and Kiska islands. Overnight, Anchorage, previously a rather lackluster little railroad town on the shores of Cook Inlet, mushroomed in size as military construction workers, soldiers, and airmen swarmed in to build and maintain airfields, ports, forts, and other installations. The same thing happened at Fairbanks and, to a lesser extent, along the southeast coast at Ketchikan, Juneau, and at other points. Fearing a submarine attack on the unprotected Alaskan coast, the military ordered construction of the "Alcan" Highway (now the Alaska Highway) from Dawson Creek, British Columbia, to Delta Junction, Alaska. Incredibly, the 1400-mile highway was completed in only eight months. It remains the only highway connecting the lower forty-eight states to the forty-ninth.

The Japanese never reached the mainland. They were repulsed finally at a cost of 2,500 American lives. When the war ended, many wartime residents stayed on, joined by later arrivals hired to construct and maintain newly authorized cold-war military installations. The long era of neglect was over. The growth of the postwar population brought an expanding and more diversified economy and, predictably, ever-increasing demands on Alaska's resources. Fishing remained the territory's primary source of income; mining, once a mainstay of the economy, declined drastically, following a trend that had started before the war. Among the new or expanding industries were construction, tourism, and logging. There was also some speculation that Alaska might contain substantial gas and oil reserves, but in that fuel-rich era the oil companies had little incentive to find out.

During this period, the drive to make Alaska the forty-ninth state was rapidly gaining momentum. Alaskans were dissatisfied with the territorial government, which was unrepresentative, unresponsive, and ineffective. Alaskans had no hand in electing the governor, who was appointed by and responsible to the Secretary of the Interior, no voice in

Malemute Native. From *Travels and Adventures in the Territory of Alaska:* Frederick Whymper (1869).

the day-to-day decisions about the territory's future, which were made in faraway Washington, and no say about where their tax monies went. They couldn't even pass bond issues for capital improvements. Even so, not all Alaskans wanted statehood. A few thought Alaska's tiny population (less than 200,000) together with unproved economic resources were simply too limited to afford the costs of becoming a state at that time. (Of course, the Alaska canned salmon industry was adamant in its opposition to statehood fearing, quite correctly, that it would lose its stranglehold over fisheries.) But the overwhelming majority favored statehood. On 30 June 1958 the United States Senate passed the statehood bill that the House of Representatives had enacted previously. Alaskans ratified the admissions bill by a vote of 40,452 to 7,010. President Eisenhower signed the bill into law, and on 3 January 1959 Alaska became the forty-ninth state.

The Alaskan panhandle looks as if it should be part of British Columbia, but because it was claimed and settled by the Russians, it became United States territory along with the rest of Alaska. Here, the coast range drops precipitously into the sea; its submerged valleys form deep, glacier-fed fjords, and its foothills shape the islands of the famous Inner Passage. But despite the mountains, the glaciers, and the deep blue water of the passage, the overwhelming impression that most visitors take away with them is of lush green forest. Everywhere on the islands and on the mountainsides, the dense rainforest of spruce, hemlock, pines, and cedar bears witness to the region's moist maritime climate. Sometimes the mountains rise gently from sea level to elevations of three to five thousand feet, but other times they seem to leap out of the water, great granite giants whose heads are lost in the clouds. Down their flanks creep hundreds of glaciers, some of them filling entire valleys and running to the water's edge, where chunks of ice are set adrift on the sea. The icebergs vary in size from some no bigger than pine cones to others that dwarf the fishing boats that ply these waters.

North of the panhandle lies the enormous Malaspina Glacier, the largest in North America outside the polar regions. Its size, estimated at some 1,500 square miles, exceeds by almost half again that of the entire state of Rhode Island. A former publicity director of the state's travel-promotion agency years ago despaired of ever getting a single picture of the entire glacier. "No photographer we assigned to the task," he reports, "was ever able to get high enough to take in its entire sprawling length and width." The Malaspina, after all, is really too immense for most of us to comprehend. We are better off, if it is glaciers we require, to turn south to Glacier Bay National Monument, situated just north and west of Juneau. Here is ice on a scale that invites rather than repels further exploration. The setting is superb: icy peaks overlook the fjord-like bay into which tumble magnificent glaciers, their sheer faces forming immense white cliffs rising above the green water. In the upper end of the bay, ice rivers descend from thousands of feet to the water's edge, where enormous chunks of the glacial faces break off and crash into the sea, their separation announced by thunder-like explosions that echo off the surrounding mountains.

It is not hard to understand why the Indians of this region regarded the glaciers, indeed all of the bay, in awe and fear. Their legends and stories tell of individuals, and even entire parties, trapped and engulfed by the massive icebergs that abound in these waters. One legend—very possibly based on fact—tells that the original founders of present-day Hoonah relocated from within the bay to their current site after a relentless onslaught of the ice engulfed their older village. But that was long ago, when the glaciers of Glacier Bay covered far more territory than they do now. They are now in steady retreat, back up the inlets that empty into the bay. When George Vancouver explored these coasts for the British crown, the entire region was covered by an ice sheet that even enveloped some of the mountains. When John Muir first visited the bay in 1879, the glacier that now bears his name was more than twenty-five miles longer than it is today. The area around Bartlett Cover, which is not far from the entrance to Glacier Bay, was covered with ice as recently as 1794. Today the land around Bartlett Cove is given over to mature stands of the same forest that drapes the coast farther south.

Parrot auk. From *Report of the Steamer Corwin in the Arctic Ocean, 1884:* U. S. Gov't Pub. (1889).

The retreating ice of Glacier Bay provides a valuable glimpse into the recent geological past of the entire panhandle region. For at one time, this entire coast lay beneath an immense ice cap. At Glacier Bay we can read the story of the retreating ice and advancing forest. Yet even here, in the largest unit of the National Park System, the powerful mining interests that dominate Alaskan politics have had their way. In 1936, only eleven years after Glacier Bay was declared a national monument, the mining lobby succeeded in persuading Congress to open the area to prospecting. Since that time, efforts to exclude mining and to preserve the area—even to make it a national park—have met with determined, articulate, high-powered resistance by mining interests, the state, and vocal members of the Alaskan business community.

Such forces oppose any legislation that would close even the most unlikely lands to prospecting and mining. Other states have survived their gold rushes—California, South Dakota, Colorado—but only Alaska seems destined to endure its gold rush indefinitely. One has to appreciate the avidity of Alaska's contemporary prospectors to understand why it is so difficult to secure protection even for the most splendid display of ice and ocean in the nation.

In the panhandle, however, fish and forests, not minerals, are the most important economic resources of the region. The salmon fishery has already been severely damaged by past misuses, and the forest resource is in danger of similar despoilation. A half-century hence, will the magnificent islands of the panhandle still boast their luxuriant stands of tall natural timber? Or will they become mere stump patches or sterile stands of second growth? Are Alaska's forests being properly managed?

Most of the panhandle lies within the boundaries of the Tongass National Forest, the largest forest in the nation. After ninety years of American jurisdiction, until the mid 1950s the Tongass and the Chugach of south-central Alaska, Alaska's only other national forest, emerged virtually intact. Here or there, a small sawmill or two had taken a few acres; a number of small village projects had removed a few more; even the military had cut small acreages in one place or another. But for the most part man's impact on the forests was negligible.

Then, in 1954 came Alaska's first pulpmill operation, on an 8.25-billion-board-foot sale area leased to Ketchikan Pulp Company.

Lanius cristatus, young. From *The Arctic Cruise of the Steamer Corwin, 1881:* U. S. Gov't Pub. (1883).

Shortly thereafter Alaska's second mill, owned by the Alaska Lumber and Pulp Company, began similar operations at Sitka in the middle panhandle. This company, wholly owned by Japanese investors, has exported virtually all of its cut to Japan and is reported to have paid few (if any) income taxes to the State of Alaska. In the nearly two decades since it chipped its first log and dissolved the fibers into pulp, the firm has apparently shown a net loss each year in its fiscal reports to the state, sufficient to make its tax obligation minimal. Finally, in 1965 the Forest Service made its third and last major sale in Alaska, a whopping 8.75-billion-board-feet of the Tongass Forest to St. Regis Paper Company—in the largest such sale in the history of the U. S. Forest Service. St. Regis later backed out, and in 1968 the lease was awarded to the second highest bidder, Champion Papers, now known as Champion International. Champion agreed to pay the price that originally had been offered by St. Regis: $5.65 per thousand board feet. In December 1969, after more than a year of studying available plant sites, Champion announced that it would build a $100-million pulp and lumber complex at Berners Bay, some forty miles north of Juneau.

Shortly thereafter, two conservation organizations and one individual sued the Forest Service in federal court, seeking to stop the sale and the construction of the pulpmill. In filing the suit, lawyers for the Sierra Club, the Sitka Conservation Society, and Alaskan master big game guide Karl Lane of Juneau contended that the Forest Service had failed to adequately consider values other than timber cutting in the one-million-acre sale area; these included recreation, watershed, wildlife, and wilderness. The plaintiffs also contended that the sale came under the provisions of the National Environmental Protection Act (N.E.P.A.) of 1969, and that the Forest Service had failed to meet requirements of the act, in particular the requirement to submit an environmental impact statement of the effects of the sale. Finally, the suit contended that the sale violated the laws limiting the purposes for which national forests may be established and administered. The major purpose of the sale, said the conservationists, was to establish a new industrial enterprise, the products of which would be used not by the people of the United States, but by those of Japan.

The future of the Tongass Forest—the scenery, the wildlife, the trees—lies with the courts, but Alaskans who favor the timber sale would do well to remember the lesson of the salmon fisheries. In fifty years, if the slopes of Admiralty Island and the adjoining mainland are crisscrossed with logging roads or patterned artificially with unnatural patches of newly-cut stump lands, new growth, later growth, and —sometimes—no growth at all, what will then support the region's economy? Fishing? Not likely, unless strict conservation measures are applied at once and rigorously adhered to. Tourism? Even less likely. The thousands who visit the panhandle each year come to see the forest and the wildlife. They will not come to see clearcut slopes; they can see those back home. Many fishermen also look with considerable apprehension at the logging alongside many salmon streams throughout the region. A resolution from the 1972 Grand Camp Convention of the Alaska Native Brotherhood, the state's oldest and largest Indian organization, notes that "logging, specifically tree falling, is still causing logs to be felled across salmon streams, causing harm to the normal flow of the streams." More bluntly, but echoing the same concern, a grizzled old fisherman on the dock at Ketchikan's Thomas Basin remarks; "It'll be a helluva note if we pump up one resource, like loggin', and screw up another resource like fishin' in the process."

The panhandle region is still dependent on the diminishing bounty of the sea, and panhandle fleets account for 20 percent of the total catch in Alaska. Anyone who has taken a ferry or steamer through the Inside Passage will recall the colorful fishing boats that share the waters—purse seiners, halibut boats, gillnetters, and trollers, some of them fast and sleek, others huffing, puffing, and dingy from age and disrepair. Yet in less than a century the fishing industry has managed to nearly wreck a resource that sustained the local Indians for thousands of years. The sea was generous, the land bountiful, and life in general so easy that these peoples developed one of the most sophisticated and affluent cultures of all the North American Indians.

Until recently, the sea also provided white Alaskans with their largest source of dollars and employment. Even today, when the fisheries have been so badly depleted, the catch contributes more than $200-million a year to the Alaskan economy. But in southeast Alaska, as well as in the Bristol Bay red salmon grounds and in the Gulf of Alaska, too many fishermen are harvesting the resource. No one is any longer able to make a decent living from fishing because too many people are going after too few fish. Alaska's fish-management biologists are each year subjected to increasing pressures to open up the fishery to longer seasons and higher catch limits.

Alaska's commercial fisheries face problems of almost crisis proportions. The salmon runs in Bristol Bay on Alaska's west coast, once the greatest in the world, have been disastrously low in recent years. Poorer runs are forecast for the future, so poor that it may be necessary to close the bay entirely to commercial fishing in order to let the runs build again to their former volume. In southeast and south-central Alaska the fishing has also been generally poor. Only the ever-increasing price for his product has kept many a fishermen from going belly-up like the catch. What, or who, is to blame for the decreased runs? Some fishermen, seeking easy answers, wrongly place the blame on natural predators such as whales, sea lions, bears, or even eagles. Others blame the foreign fleets of large, efficient "factory ships" that have intruded into Alaskan fisheries. Japanese, Russian, and Korean vessels have been seized and brought to trial for fishing in Alaskan waters, or for otherwise breaking international fisheries agreements between their countries and the United States. Many violators, probably most, have not been apprehended. Biologists point out that especially bitter weather conditions over the past years may well have contributed to poor fish production. Few fishermen until recently however, have considered a significant fact that the state must explore more carefully: Alaskan fishermen are catching more fish than the resource can bear. Pressures to bend or totally reverse sound management decisions are constant—from political groups and individuals, from economic interests, and from well-meaning but sometimes misinformed citizen groups.

There is one strong ray of hope. Alaska's legislature—at the urging of fishermen's groups themselves—has established a unique new policy called "Limited Entry." The policy seeks to limit the number of

Ciceronia pusilla, adult, breeding plumage. From *The Arctic Cruise of the Steamer Corwin, 1881:* U. S. Gov't Pub. (1883).

fishermen in Alaskan waters hopefully to the carrying capacity of the resource. Necessarily complex and time consuming, the machinery of limited entry is only now entering its initial phases. The test of the effectiveness of the program will come when the state's Limited Entry Commission determines how many fishermen will be allowed permits to fish in given regions, and how many will be denied entry to the fishery. When these tough decisions are made (or, tragically, not made) Alaskans will know whether their fisheries will continue to be overcrowded and overfished or whether they can look forward to a time of renewed runs and a healthy resource.

Everywhere in Alaska increasing numbers of people are making greater demands on the land and resources of the state. Up till now Alaska has been able to get along without putting severe limitations on what people could and could not do, but that carefree frontier past is over. If the state is to retain its wilderness beauty and its abundant resources, it will have to plan for the future. Otherwise, fifty or one hundred years from now, the minerals and forests, along with the fisheries and wildlife, will become fond memories. Even the North-Slope oil will not last forever. Alaskans have experienced enough boom-and-bust periods. Tomorrow's economy should be based on long-term management of the land and resources, not on the get-in-get-out schemes that have left Alaskans poorer in the past.

If one were to ask any ten people on the streets of Anchorage to name Alaska's greatest resource for the future, nine of them would say "oil." In logging and milling towns like Ketchikan the answer would probably be "timber." And in small coastal towns such as Petersburg or Kodiak, residents might still think Alaska's depleted fisheries are the resource that will prove to be the strongest base for Alaska's economy. Although all these resources will continue to prove important, the one least mentioned—wilderness—may ultimately provide one of the greatest self-perpetuating resources of all. Henry Gannet, a former chief of the United States Geological Survey pointed out the importance of wilderness in Alaska as long ago as 1904.

"One of the chief assets of Alaska, if not the greatest," Gannet wrote, "is the scenery. There are glaciers, mountains, fjords elsewhere, but nowhere else on earth is there such abundance and magnificence of mountain, fjord and glacier scenery. For thousands of miles the coast is a continuous panorama. For one Yosemite of California, Alaska has hundreds. The mountains and glaciers of the Cascade Range are duplicated and a thousand fold exceeded in Alaska. The Alaska coast is to become the showplace of the entire earth. . . . [Alaska's] grandeur is more valuable than the gold or the fish or the timber for it will never be exhausted."

Although occasionally marked (many would say marred) by acres of clearcut logging, which comes all the way down to the beachline, and by other evidences of the twentieth-century use and abuse, most of the 30,000-mile coastal panorama that Gannett spoke of survives today, largely as he saw it at the turn of the century and as nature fashioned it aeons ago. The waters in all but a few of Alaska's lakes and streams and saltwater fjords remain relatively pure and unpolluted. The state's magnificent mountains, with only a few exceptions, stand ungouged. Yet for all this, Alaska still contains no officially designated wilderness areas and only four units in the national park system—Mt. McKinley National

Park, Glacier Bay National Monument, Katmai National Monument, and Sitka National Historic Park, which commemorates the old Russian settlement. Efforts to establish additional units have met consistent opposition from mining and timber interests in the state.

Katmai National Monument and Mt. McKinley National Park are situated generally in the south-central region of Alaska: Katmai on the Alaska Peninsula, and McKinley in the heart of the Alaska Range, which divides the south-central region from the colder interior. The region is bordered on the east by the magnificent Wrangell Mountains. In ruggedness, wildlife, and sheer scenic splendor, the Wrangells equal or surpass any other mountain wilderness in North America. Anywhere else in the United States, this range would have long ago been set aside, at least in part, as a national park.

Katmai National Monument on the Alaska Peninsula is possibly the least spoiled unit in the National Park System. Accessible only by air, it is rarely visited except by those who crave a unique wilderness experience. For the Valley of the Ten Thousand Smokes is unlike any other place on the continent. Once green and forested, today the valley looks like the surface of the moon. In 1912 Mt. Novarupta erupted, hurling more than seven cubic miles of pumice and rock into the atmosphere and pouring a river of white-hot ash into the valley, sometimes to a depth of 700 feet. No growing thing survived. When the fiery avalanche subsided, hot gases escaped into the air through small vents in the earth, creating the 10,000 smokes that gave the valley its name.

A man of Oonalashka. From *Voyage to the Pacific Ocean:* Cap't James Cook (1789).

Today all but a few of the smokes are extinguished, but the valley remains one of the most starkly desolate spots on the planet—and one of the most strangely beautiful. The now compacted ash is so acidic that practically no grasses, shrubs, or trees can live in the valley. Park rangers complain that their boot bindings become eaten through by the action of the acid. So one is startled to come upon the footprints of a moose or even a brown bear in this moonscape, far from any source of food. One is tempted to hope that they, like people, come to the Valley of Ten Thousand Smokes for a moment of solitude that each years grows increasingly uncommon, even in Alaska.

Katmai is the second largest unit in the entire National Park System, exceeded in size only by Glacier Bay. Both monuments encompass almost three million acres, most of which are wilderness of doubtful commercial potential. Yet proposals to classify these lands as wilderness areas have been consistently opposed by the state government, chambers of commerce, and business and industry spokesmen—the same coalition that opposes wilderness designation everywhere in Alaska. So too, they have opposed extensions to Mt. McKinley National Park and the creation of a Wrangell Mountains National Park and a Gates of the Arctic National Park in the Central Brooks Range.

The grandeur and spectacle of the Wrangell Mountains is on a scale that is unmatched even in Alaska. Various writers have called these mountains the "jewels" of central Alaska, and even a distant view of the range, such as that seen from the Richardson Highway en route from Valdez to Fairbanks, tells why. The glistening peaks, two of which exceed 16,000 feet, rise abruptly from the surrounding lowlands. The roof of the range is an icy wilderness, scoured by glaciers and lying perennially beneath a mantle of snow, but at lower elevations lakes and meadows and valleys form a lush parkland that supports an abundance and variety of wildlife unsurpassed in Alaska.

For years, conservationists in Alaska have urged the creation of a Wrangell Mountains National Park. In December 1973, when the Secretary of the Interior announced his federal land withdrawals in accordance with the terms of the Alaska Native Claims Settlement Act, the Secretary's proposal did indeed contain a recommendation for the establishment of a Wrangell-St. Elias National Park. This park, some 8.64 million acres in size, would cover a portion of the Wrangell range and a portion as well of the St. Elias mountains to the southeast. But here's the rub: The secretary also recommended that a 5.5 million acre Wrangell National Forest also be created—a two-part forest to be located on two sides of the proposed park. The trouble with this, say knowledgeable conservationists, is that the land recommended for Forest Service jurisdiction is among the most valuable, from the standpoint of park values, in the range. Further, the region contains almost no commercial timber stands—by the Forest Service's own admission. What these lands do contain, of course, are minerals. Between 1911 and 1938, Kennecott Copper took more than a billion pounds of high-grade copper from the Wrangells. The prospect of future bonanzas of this scale assured that at least a substantial portion of the present wilderness would be designated for national forest rather than national park status. But the final decision will rest with Congress, which must pass on Interior's recommendations by 1978, and conservationists will not rest in their attempts to persuade Congress that the Wrangells should be managed not for commercial gain, but for all time.

"It is in the Wrangells," said one Alaskan after hiking and tenting in the area, "that the story of America's commitment to do what is environmentally right in Alaska will be told. If we fail, if we try to make the Wrangells all things for all people, for all purposes, then we will have added, in Alaska, still another sorry entry to America's list of ecological failures.

"If, however, Alaskans and the Secretary of the Interior and the Congress act in a way to protect the scenic and wilderness values that exist in the Wrangells, if we protect those values for all time and for all generations to come, then the prospects for Alaska's and America's environmental future will look bright indeed."

For now, Alaska's only national park is Mt. McKinley, which is located some 150 miles north of Anchorage in the heart of the Alaska Range. At 20,320 feet, McKinley is by far the tallest peak in North America, but what often impresses the visitor more than its height is its enormous bulk. Rising from a base elevation between one and two thousand feet, it dwarfs everything around it, including the nearby peaks of the Alaska Range. It seems itself like an entire range, an impression that is reinforced from the air. From a plane, the mountain shows itself to be a jumbled chaos of hundreds of clawlike peaks and crags and knife-sharp ridges, of monstrous ice walls, rock barriers, hanging glaciers, and rock-hard snow fields. Separating the crags from one another are valley glaciers so numerous that only the grandest have been given names. It seems incredible that scores of climbers have successfully ascended McKinley's twin summits.

The park exists because of the mountain, but its popularity as

A woman of Oonalashka. From *Voyage to the Pacific Ocean:* Cap't James Cook (1784).

Alaska's number-one tourist attraction lies as much in its abundant and often-sighted wildlife as in its remarkable topography. Here, the chances of seeing grizzly bears, wolves, caribou, moose, beaver, wolverines, martens, and mountain sheep are better than anywhere else in Alaska. While some of these species are extremely shy, others, such as sheep, caribou, and bear, are often seen from the park road. The number of animals that venture near the highway has noticeably increased since the Park Service began to restrict auto traffic to the number of vehicles that can be accommodated in the park campgrounds. The Park Service also runs a shuttle bus within the park, which allows campers and backpackers to travel through various parts of the park unencumbered by the automobile.

North of the curving arc of the Alaska Range stretches a vast region of indeterminate boundaries that Alaskans neatly summarize as the interior, not so much a region as a state of mind. Except for Fairbanks, which at 50,000, is the state's second-largest community, the interior is sparsely populated—an occasional Indian village, a community of trappers and fishermen, a scattering of wilderness cabins. Its brief summers, sometimes bitterly cold winters, and miles of muskeg and mosquitoes have been sufficient to keep most Alaskans, like the Russians before them, huddled near the comparatively balmy southern coasts. Many Alaskans and Alaska visitors have driven and flown to Fairbanks, but few have explored much beyond except to a few "package tour" destinations. For one thing, many communities are isolated by snow for most of the year. Many more are accessible only by plane. As one might expect, there is a tendency in Alaska to overestimate the vastness of the interior and underestimate, except in terms of prospecting, its value. This tendency leads in turn to the attitude that it doesn't much matter what you do to the region because there's so much of it. As is so often the case, attitudes are frozen into policy by people who are only vaguely familiar with the facts.

Typical of this process was the Army Corps of Engineers' scheme to flood the Yukon Flats a few years back. The now infamous but unbuilt Rampart Dam proposed for the Yukon River would have flooded a portion of the interior larger than Lake Erie. Through these lowlands, the Yukon and its tributaries grow lazy after their rough and tumble journey out of the mountains. They spread out over the flat valley, breaking into scores of meanders and backwaters edged everywhere with marsh. Covering thousands of square miles, this wetland habitat is one of the major breeding grounds for North American waterfowl, as are the Innoko, Koyukuk, and Kanuti flats and the Yukon Delta farther downriver. Flooding the Yukon Flats would have tinkered with the ecology of a continent, for it would have seriously reduced the waterfowl population that summers in Alaska but winters in the south. However, to the dammers and developers, ignorant of such relationships between wildlife and the land, the Yukon Flats were merely swampy, bug-ridden, scrub-timbered wastelands. The Army Corps of Engineers reasoned that building the dam in country so vast as Alaska's interior would not incur a significant loss. That false impression of infinite bigness and limited worth almost spawned a disaster.

The Rampart Dam battle was Alaska's first major environmental conflict that captured the imagination of the entire nation. The ill-

"While descending the stream on the 24th, late in the forenoon, we saw a large buck moose swim from one of the many islands to the mainland just back of us, having probably, as the hunter would say, 'gotten our scent.' I never comprehended what immense noses these animals have until I got a good profile view of this big fellow and although over half a mile away, his nose looked as if he had been rooting the island and was trying to carry away the greatest part of it on the end of his snout. The great palmated horns above, the broad "throat-latch" before, combined with the huge nose and powerful shoulders, make one think that this animal might tilt forward on his head from sheer gravity, so little is there apparently at the other end to counterbalance these masses."

FREDERICK SCHWATKA, *A Summer in Alaska.*

advised project was shelved, but more recently, developers and conservationists have bitterly fought over the future of the several great breeding grounds along the Yukon River. Conservationists want them included in the system of national wildlife refuges, but prospectors and mining interests demand that they be kept open to mining.

Most of the interior is still untrammeled wilderness. It abounds with wildlife, the most notable of which is the caribou, which gathers in enormous herds numbering in the tens of thousands. Grizzlies, black-bears, lynx, and wolves are more common than people in some areas. Water and forage are abundant in the interior, as they were during the last Ice Age, when the region's vast prairies supported numerous herds of mammals. North of Fairbanks fossil bear skulls have been unearthed that measure twice the size of today's Kodiak brown bears, which are the largest land carnivores in the world. Other digs have turned up the remains of mastodons, hairy mammoths, giant elk, saber-toothed cats, woolly rhinoceros, moose, horses, and ancient bison. Some of these animals may have lured the first men across the land bridge from Asia and drew them into the great heartland of Alaska. The Athabascan Indians, inhabitants of this land for centuries, have always been hunters and fishermen, and for the most part remain so today.

The interior is not without its mountains, but it is largely a land of rolling hills and broad, flat lowlands, of countless ponds, marshes, and serpentine streams. The land is not as spectacular as that of the Brooks Range to the north or as the mountains and forests of the south, but for many Indians, trappers, and prospectors it is the finest place on earth. They do not look forward to a time when the region may be criss-crossed with highways or dotted with towns. The interior has a beauty more subtle than that of mountain and forest, and lies not so much in what is seen as in the all-pervasive mood of wildness and freedom. In the summer and early fall the interior comes alive with color. Roadside fields blaze with the red glow of the fireweed and the rainbow colors of thousands of wildflowers, out for a brief fling before the long winter settles over them. As the season proceeds, the brilliant hues of flowers are replaced by reds, oranges, and yellows of dying autumn leaves. Finally, all is white; the summer sun is a warm memory.

But even on the warmest summer days, a bit of winter lurks just below the ground, for most of the interior lowlands, like the Arctic tundra, are underlain with permafrost, a permanently frozen stratum of earth and ice. In some areas the original freezing of a piece of ground may have taken place as long as a million years ago. Most present permafrost probably dates from the last major advances of ice, some tens of thousands of years ago. Permafrost is responsible for the seemingly endless miles of muskeg bogs that cover the interior lowlands. In summer, melting snow and ice are trapped at and just below the surface of the ground because of the impermeable layer of permafrost only a few feet below. Permafrost is also responsible for the well-preserved fossils that are found in Alaska. Nature's own deep freeze preserves creatures ancient and not so ancient, at least if you can believe Willie Brown, the tour guide at Nome, who tells about a local widow who had occasion to look into her dead husband's casket years after he had been buried in the permafrost of the local cemetery. According to Willie, "The old boy was just as purty as he ever was."

Permafrost can be a few feet deep, or it can seem almost endless. It would be hard to find an interior Alaskan outside of the urban areas who has not had to deal with it. It influences his ground water supply; it inhibits his septic tank and drain field; and if he is one of the few old-timers who still tries to muck out a living from placer mining, it effectively blocks any useful work he might do until he can thaw the ground to be worked, usually by pressure-pumping quantities of water into the area. Many are the engineers and architects who have underestimated and miscalculated permafrost and its disastrous thrusting and twisting effects on the house foundations, pilings, and other subsurface structures. Floors under big buildings and small rise, fall, buckle, fold, and split, as do roadways, airport runways, water lines, and sewer systems.

And, say concerned environmentalists, so will the projected trans-Alaska hot oil pipeline unless every technological safeguard known to man is incorporated into the construction of the facility. Environmentalists also fear the possible adverse effects the pipeline may have on migrating patterns of wildlife of the region, especially the great herds of caribou, which twice each year travel hundreds of miles to their summer and winter ranges.

From its point of origin near Prudhoe Bay, the pipeline will first run south across miles of tundra and then over the rugged Brooks Range before reaching the broad lowlands of the Alaskan interior. The Brooks Range, which runs east-west across Alaska, lies mostly north of the Arctic Circle and divides the waters that flow south into the interior and from there to the Pacific, from those that flow north across the North Slope into the Arctic Ocean. Generally speaking, the tallest peaks in the Brooks Range lie to the east, in the area of the Arctic National Wildlife Range, where Mt. Chamberlin, Mt. Isto, and Mt. Michelson reach heights of approximately 9,000 feet. At the western end of the range the mountains average 3,000 to 4,000 feet. Although the Brooks Range is not the highest on the continent, or even in the state, many of its peaks, especially the towering, granite Arrigetch Peaks of the central range, are considered by mountaineers to be among the most rugged, precipitous, and challenging in North America.

As readers of conservation and wilderness literature will know, the Brooks Range, especially the central portion, is Robert Marshall country. As late as the 1930s this land was still largely unmapped and unexplored, at least by white men. Marshall and his companions struck out into the heart of the range, discovering such notable peaks as Mt. Doonerak, Boreal Mountain, and Frigid Crags. Marshall named Doonerak, the dark and brooding devil mountain, after an Eskimo word dealing with spirits. He dubbed Boreal Mountain and Frigid Crags, which rise on either side of the north fork of the Koyukuk River, the Gates of the Arctic and proposed that this entire portion of the Brooks Range be preserved in a Gates of the Arctic National Park. Now, more than forty years later, conservationists are actively pushing for the park, but, as in the Wrangells, mining interests have so far had their way.

Beyond the Brooks Range lies the North Slope, a broad treeless plain between the mountains and the Arctic Ocean. The North Slope is so flat that even a small mound (or abandoned oil drum) takes on the appearance of height all out of proportion to its actual size. Early accounts tell of explorers believing they had sighted mountains east of the Colville River only to discover on closer inspection that the supposed range were merely sand dunes. Tens of thousands of bogs and ponds dot these flatlands, making summertime overland travel in a straight line impossible. The ground is springy, yielding to the step, and tricky to walk through. The vegetation forms a thick mat of interwoven plants—berries, lichens, wildflowers—usually in miniature, and always colorful.

But tear up a piece of that spongy arctic earth, scrape off a layer of plant cover, and the regenerative process, which elsewhere might begin in weeks, may well take decades, or may never take place at all. For the tundra is in many ways an Arctic desert where precipitation is slight and the progress of vegetation slow. The North Slope is at once harsh and fragile—again like the desert—a paradox that is neatly demonstrated by the attitudes of two different men who have both lived and worked on the North Slope. The first, a scientist, told the Resources Committee of the Alaska House of Representatives that "this tundra . . . is so delicate, so fragile, that if you drive across it in even a light vehicle, let alone a monstrously heavy rig like a bulldozer, your tracks will likely remain an unhealed sore on the surface for a decade or longer." The second man, an oil company lobbyist, told a young legislative employee: "That place is one hell-froze-over country. You take a day when it's fifty or sixty below, and the wind is blowing forty or fifty per, cutting right through your parka no matter how much insulation you've got in it, and the snow's flying so thick you can't see the mitten on the end of your arm . . . well, you know you're working in one goddam hostile environment."

Both men are quite accurate in their descriptions. The Arctic winters are long and severe. Spring does not come to this region until summer is well underway in other parts of the country. Snow in July is not rare. And just as life on the North Slope is difficult and miserable for workmen trying to set up and maintain oil rigs and camps and transportation facilities, life is equally tough for plants and grasses and wildlife. The oil development will only make it tougher.

Regardless of when and where the pipeline is constructed, life in the Arctic will never again be the isolated wilderness existence it once was. Conditions are changing not only for the flora and fauna, but also for the native peoples who have always lived on this northern land.

Of the native Alaskans, the Eskimos and Athabascan Indians, who inhabit the interior wilderness and frigid North Slope, have been least affected by the impact of modern civilization. The Athabascans traded with the coastal Indians for centuries, but they had virtually no contact with white men except fur traders and early prospectors, until the gold stampedes of the 1890s and early years of the twentieth century. Many old-timers remember when almost no one but Indians and Eskimos inhabited the interior. But with the extension of highways, the growth of Fairbanks and other interior cities, the North Slope oil boom, and the effects of the Alaska Native Claims Settlement Act, both the Eskimos and the Athabascans will be hard put in the years ahead to retain even the rudiments of their aboriginal cultures.

Contrary to what many people seem to believe, the land of the Eskimo has never been restricted to the country north of the Arctic Circle. Long ago the Eskimo lived even farther south than he does today, but even now there are settlements near Nome, on St. Lawrence and Nunivak islands, at Bethel, and at various points along the salmon-rich shores of Bristol Bay. Wherever the community is located, however, life for the Eskimo remains largely a matter of subsistence. In a few places Eskimos herd reindeer and musk ox or earn a little from the tourist trade, but these are exceptions. For the most part, the meat on the family table in a typical Eskimo home gets there because the father and sons hunt

Rhodostethia rosea, male, in winter plumage. From *The Report of the International Polar Expedition to Point Barrow, Alaska, 1882:* U. S. Gov't Pub. (1885).

A white bear. From *Sauer's Billings Expedition to the North of Russia* (1802).

caribou, moose, seal, and walrus, or because the whole family goes fishing.

Nevertheless, the old ways are dying for the Eskimos. In some areas the hunting is no longer good. There aren't as many seals or whales or polar bears as there used to be. The salmon aren't so plentiful. More and more, today's Eskimo needs cash to buy the things he needs. Yet with few exceptions, there is no source of cash in most Eskimo settlements. In many villages the biggest payroll in town may be the arrival of National Guard checks.

Life is considerably different, though not a great deal more comfortable, for the Eskimo's near relative, the Aleutian Islander, whose home is the 1,400-mile-long chain of islands stretching from the Alaskan mainland almost to Siberia. The Aleuts probably face fewer difficulties adjusting to the demands of the modern world than do the Eskimos or Indians; their initiation into the ways of the white man came 200 years ago when the first Russians used their islands as steppingstones to Alaska. Chances are good that the typical Aleut is part Russian. He probably is a commercial fisherman, unless he happens to be among those of his people who live and work for the federal government on the Pribilof Islands, where each year the Aleuts assist in the annual, treaty-sanctioned harvest of the fur seals. Despite the Aleut's knowledge of the sea and his willingness to work in one of the most savage and unpredictable fisheries in the world, his annual catch from the depleted resource does not provide a much higher standard of living than his Eskimo cousins enjoy.

The situations of the two major groups of Indians parallel those of the Aleuts and Eskimos. The coast-dwelling Tlingits fought their battle with western civilization long ago—and lost. Those that remain have already adapted to the modern world. They face far fewer problems than the

Athabascan peoples of the interior, whose rite of passage, like that of the Eskimo, has been postponed by the remoteness and harshness of their homelands. Before the coming of the white man, the Athabascans led a tough, spartan life. Some would say they still do. They live in isolated villages, enjoy few of the fruits of modern life yet increasingly feel its adverse effects in the disruption of their previous nomadic existence; they continue to rely on the seriously depleted wildlife populations, and must bear with other intrusions on their traditional ways. The Athabascans were (and to the extent that modern conditions allow, still are) hunters and fishermen. In the central and eastern portions of the interior, hunting was more important than fishing in the old days, although the increasing scarcity of game may be altering this pattern. Nearer to the coast, where rivers produced large quantities of salmon and other fish, fishing was the more important method of securing food. For many of these people, life has changed little since the first miners entered their territory in the late nineteenth century, but for others the old culture, depending largely on hunting and fishing, is rapidly disappearing along with the game.

One modern Athabascan settlement is Circle City, thus named because its residents believed it straddled the Arctic Circle. In fact, it lies about fifty miles south, although it does have the dubious distinction of being the most northern community in North America that can be reached by highway. Here life remains pretty much unchanged. Dog sleds are still not an uncommon means of transportation during the winter, and salmon fishing and hunting are still the primary economic activities of the town. For three-quarters of the year, Circle City is cut off from all surface transportation, cut off, in effect, from the interference of the modern world. "Much better, much better in winter," said one old-timer, "More quiet, more peaceful, much better."

But for increasing numbers of Indians, Aleuts, and Eskimos in recent years, village life has been much worse. Unable to carry on the old ways and ill prepared to cope with the new, many Alaskan natives have migrated to "big cities" such as Fairbanks and Anchorage, hoping to make a new life after the old had gone sour. The newly arrived Eskimo, skilled only in Arctic survival and subsistence, has virtually no chance in the relatively sophisticated urban labor market, for unemployment in Alaska's cities, especially among unskilled workers, is as high as or higher than anywhere else in the country. The native's problems do not go away; they change, becoming worse in the process because he is now cut off from both his land and his past. For these refugees of the modern world, the Alaska Native Claims Settlement Act seems like a last hope.

Whatever the act holds in store for Alaska's native peoples, its effect on the population as a whole and on the future direction of Alaskan history will be profound. It will in large part determine how much of Alaska will be developed into a northern carbon copy of the rest of the United States and how much will remain as wilderness. Secretary of the Interior Rogers C. B. Morton submitted his federal withdrawal recommendations to Congress in December 1973, but the debate over who will get what lands and what will be done with them will continue long after Congress acts on the secretary's recommendations sometime in 1978. Naturally, the partitioning of Alaska's public lands, no matter how carefully planned and executed, was bound to become, finally, a strenu-

A man of Kadiak. From *Sauer's Billings Expedition to the North of Russia* (1802).

ous political tug-of-war resulting in a compromise pleasing no one. When the Secretary of the Interior announced his recommendations, no one was happy. Conservationists objected that too many "national interest" lands were either omitted from the withdrawal list or placed under the jurisdiction of the National Forest Service, where they will be vulnerable to logging, mining, road building, and recreational development. Those who favored development argued that the government had "locked up" too many lands from development by designating them as national parks, wildlife refuges, and the like.

Alaska's population is deeply divided over what future course the state should take; whether it should begin a crash program of economic and industrial development, or whether it should strive to maintain its present wilderness character. Some Alaskans are dead set against establishing any more parks or wilderness areas, as if these somehow represented a closing of the great frontier they have so long regarded as their own. Loggers, mining associations, chambers of commerce, and the state administration all oppose wilderness withdrawals. They steadfastly regard any wilderness withdrawals as lock ups of their land, even though it was never their land but part of the public domain. When Secretary Morton announced that of the 83 million acres of national interest lands, 31.6 million acres would be set aside as national wildlife refuges and another 32.26 million as national parks and monuments, the proponents of development howled in protest, even though mining, oil, and gas development would be permitted on virtually all of the 18.8 million acres of forest lands plus 24 million of the proposed 31.5 million wildlife lands. Too, hunting would be allowed on 75 of the 83 million acres that were withdrawn. Furthermore, conservationists were quick to point out that much of the proposed national park lands consisted of glaciated mountain peaks of no conceivable commercial value, that large portions of outstanding national park candidate areas such as the Wrangell Mountains and the Central Brooks Range were turned over to the Forest Service, and that several other areas of prime importance to wildlife were either omitted from the recommendations or placed under the Forest Service's jurisdiction.

What the opponents of wilderness in Alaska fail to understand, or prefer not to understand, is that no responsible environmental groups are seeking to lock up all of Alaska, or even the greater portion of the state. The federal withdrawals make up only 23 percent of Alaska's 365 million acres, and most of the federal lands are not locked up by any definition. The State of Alaska, through the statehood act, is entitled to select more than 100 million acres of Alaska's public land, which it can use as it pleases. Alaska's native communities and corporations will select another 40 million acres. It is highly unlikely that either the state or the natives will lock up their lands.

Environmentalists are not suggesting that all of Alaska be turned into national parks and wilderness areas. What they are saying is this: Alone of all the states, Alaska remains blessed not merely with thousands or hundreds of thousands of acres of wilderness, but with tens of millions of acres—lands containing some of the most awesome, unspoiled wild forests, mountains, rivers, and lakes left on earth. For much of these lands, the highest and best use to which they could be put is wilderness. Parts of Glacier Bay National Monument, sections of Katmai National

Monument, parts of the national forests, lands on the Kenai Moose Range, certain areas in Mt. McKinley National Park, portions of the Brooks Range, and other areas like them are so magnificent in their wild, unconquered beauty, that they deserve maximum protection from any kind of development. Unborn generations of Americans will then have the opportunity to see and explore a portion of the earth left largely as nature created it.

Although many of the federal withdrawal areas, along with others that were not withdrawn despite the support of conservationists, contain commercially valuable mineral deposits and forests, they are not, as one would sometimes think from listening to mining and timber interests, the only lands so richly endowed. There remain tens of millions of acres outside the choicest scenic, wilderness, and wildlife areas that will remain open to commercial exploitation. One wonders why the opponents of wilderness protection in Alaska feel they must be able to exploit all the public domain. Even from the crassest dollars-and-cents point of view, Alaska's scenic areas should be preserved if only to maintain and encourage the state's thriving tourist industry. Each year thousands of tourists come to Alaska, not to see mining operations, clearcut forests, or pipelines, but to experience the wilderness, even if that means nothing more than a steamer cruise through the Inside Passage or a highway trip through Mt. McKinley National Park.

Alaska is America's last true wilderness, the only place left where one can re-experience the excitement of the American pioneers more than a century ago as they faced a vast, hostile, yet bountiful land. Yet like the West, the Alaska that inspires such dreams will disappear as fantasy is translated into action. The vision of abundance and unlimited opportunity blesses only the first men who cross the frontier. Those who follow must feed on memories and rest content with leftovers. Alaska is an enormous and generous land, but it is far smaller than the western states, which were subdued in less than a century at a time when the wheels of progress were wooden and slow. Unless Alaskans consider now whether they want to live in a land tamed by commerce and condemned by growth to become a carbon copy of virtually every other state, the Great Land will vanish in their lifetimes. And when Alaska's wilderness is gone, America will have no frontier.

Ursine seal. From *The Sketchbook of W. Smyth, HMS Blossom,* Beechey's Expedition to the Bering Straits (1825).

2. The Great Land

*There is one other asset of the territory not yet enumerated;
imponderable and difficult to appraise, yet one of the chief
assets of Alaska, if not the greatest. This is the scenery. There
are glaciers, mountains, fiords elsewhere, but nowhere else on
earth is there such abundance and magnificence of mountain,
fiord and glacier scenery. For thousands of miles the coast is a
continuous panorama. For one Yosemite of California, Alaska
has hundreds. The mountains and glaciers of the Cascade
Range are duplicated and a thousand fold exceeded in Alaska.
The Alaska coast is to become the show place of the entire
earth, and pilgrims not only from the United States but from
beyond the seas will throng in endless procession to see it. Its
grandeur is more valuable than the gold or the fish, or the
timber, for it will never be exhausted. This value, measured by
direct returns in money received from tourists, will be enormous; measured by health and pleasure it will be incalculable.
(1898)*

HENRY GANNETT, Harriman Alaska Expedition

. . . in these coast landscapes there is such indefinite, onleading expansiveness, such a multitude of features without apparent redundance, their lines graduating delicately into one another in endless succession, while the whole is so fine, so tender, so ethereal, that all penwork seems hopelessly unavailing.
JOHN MUIR, *Travels in Alaska*

A Blue Day Breaking, WILBUR MILLS

Myriad Islands, PHILIP HYDE

Lichen, PHILIP HYDE

It is impossible ever to evaluate just how much beauty adds to what is worth while in existence. I would hazard as my opinion that beautiful surroundings have a fundamental bearing on most people's enjoyment. Consequently, I believe that . . . life is made richer by the overpowering loveliness of the Arctic Wilderness.
ROBERT MARSHALL, *Arctic Village*

Leaf detail, Fall, PHILIP HYDE

Arrigetch Creek, WILBUR MILLS

Moss, North Fork, Koyukuk River, WILBUR MILLS

Glacier, Arrigetch Peaks, WILBUR MILLS

The powers of water are immeasurable. In the form of ice it can chisel rock as effectively as steel. Unloosed in a river it can slice through layers of volcanic ash like a knife through cake. Meandering in a shady stream, it can make the home for green growing things . . .
PEGGY WAYBURN

Alsek River, EDGAR WAYBURN

Ruth Glacier, Mt. McKinley, EDGAR WAYBURN

Our national parks, here in the north, are set aside, not only for Alaskans, or for Americans, but for all humanity. To preserve the delicate charm and the wilderness of the region our thoughts must be guided by a morality encompassing the spiritual welfare of the universe.
ADOLPH MURIE, *Mammals of Mount McKinley National Park*

Stream Grass, TIM THOMPSON

The song of a river ordinarily means the tune that waters play on rock, root, and rapid . . .
ALDO LEOPOLD
Sand County Almanac

Summer Stream, WILBUR MILLS

Arrigetch Tarn and Peaks, WILBUR MILLS

*Two things constantly baffle and mislead the eye
in . . . Alaska . . . size and distance. . . . The eye says it is
three miles to such a point and it turns out six; or that
the front of yonder glacier is a hundred feet high and it is
two hundred or more. . . . The wonderfully clear air
probably had something to do with the illusion. Forms
were so distinct that one fancied them near at hand
when they were not.*
JOHN BURROUGHS, *Harriman Alaska Expedition*

47

Looking South to the Brooks Range, WILBUR MILLS

Arrigetch Peaks, WILBUR MILLS

*All was peace
and strength
and immensity
and coordination
and freedom.*
ROBERT MARSHALL
Alaska Wilderness

Sitka Shore, TIM THOMPSON

Beaufort Lagoon, WILBUR MILLS

The scenery of the ocean, however sublime in vast ex-
panse, seems far less beautiful to us dry-shod animals
than that of the land seen only in comparatively small
patches; but when we contemplate the whole globe as
one great dewdrop, striped and dotted with continents
and islands, . . . the whole universe appears as an infinite
storm of beauty.
JOHN MUIR, *Travels in Alaska*

Tidal Flats, Turnagin Arm, TIM THOMPSON

We learn and learn,
but never know all,
about the smallest,
humblest thing.
D'ARCY THOMPSON
On Growth and Form

Shoreline near Gustavus, TIM THOMPSON

Packing Out, OLAF SOOT

. . . *no comfort, no security, no invention,
no brilliant thought which the modern
world had to offer could provide half the
elation of the days spent in the little-
explored, uninhabited world of the arctic
wilderness.*
ROBERT MARSHALL, *Alaska Wilderness*

We come to watch; to catch a glimpse of the primeval. We come close to the tundra flowers, the lichens, and the animal life. Each of us will take some inspiration home: a touch of the tundra will enter our lives—and, deep inside, make of us all poets and kindred spirits.
ADOLPH MURIE, *Mammals of Mount McKinley National Park*

Cottonwood Leaves, WILBUR MILLS

Fireweed in Fall, TIM THOMPSON

The flowers crowded hard upon this ice. On the higher ground they bloomed, had their growth, and went to seed in June and July. Those plants under the ice had to wait. Then, as the ice melted away, flowers would come up in the newly released earth. Late in summer some of these were bravely in bloom, when those of the same species on higher ground had bloomed long ago and were now in seed!
OLAUS J. MURIE
Journeys to the Far North

Tundra, Fall, WILBUR MILLS

Dry Stream Bed, WILBUR MILLS

All men who come here live but a part of the truth; tomorrow will not be the same as today. The true reality of this land is change. The snowflake melts. Mountains crumble.
JOHN MILTON
Nameless Valleys,
Shining Mountains

South Side Mendenhall Glacier, TIM THOMPSON

I had given this venture much thought. Here was a part of the North at stake—a symbol of the whole circumpolar Arctic. What should mankind do with it? . . . we tend to forget the fundamental aspects of nature as presented to us on this planet. Will we have the patience to observe and try to understand what the northern part of the earth has to offer?
Olaus J. Murie, *Journeys to the Far North*

North Slope, WILBUR MILLS

*I was again installed in the wilderness; a sense of
deep contentment stole over me as, a little later, I
sat looking out on the calm water of the beautiful
bay—ducks lazily floating about; geese flying low
to their feeding-grounds, making the air vibrate
with the music of their honking; gulls screaming;
large flocks of shore birds skirting the beaches,
while behind, in the woods, there sounded now
and then the sweet song of a warbler.*
CHARLES SHELDON, *The Wilderness of the
North Pacific Coast Islands*

Copper River Delta, PHILIP HYDE

As the first few days went by, I kept thinking about why we two had come back up here. We were both accustomed to living in the northland, and I suppose much of our lives is influenced by environment. But there must be an attitude inherent in us that strives for expression. And I think there is another deep-seated impulse—one that is emerging throughout the world—to try to improve our culture. There is in all of us the urge to share beauty and freedom with other sensitive people.
OLAUS J. MURIE, *Journeys to the Far North*

Mt. Blackburn from across the Copper River, PHILIP HYDE

Tundra, Mt. McKinley National Park, PHILIP HYDE

It was a very novel experience, this walking over the tundra; its vastness, its uniformity, its solitude, its gentleness, its softness of contour, its truly borean character—the truncated hills and peaks on the near horizon suggesting huge earthworks, the rounded and curved elevations like the backs of prostrate giants turned up to the sun, and farther off the high serrated snow-streaked ranges on the remote horizon to the north—all made up a curious and unfamiliar picture.

That lift heavenward of the solid crust of the earth, that aspiration of the insensate rocks, that effort of the whole range, as it were, to carry one peak into heights where all may not go . . . it stands there in a kind of serene astronomic solitude and remoteness . . . a vision that always shakes the heart of the beholder.
JOHN BURROUGHS, *Harriman Alaska Expedition*

Brooks Range Peak, BOB WALDROP

Ash Flow, Katmai National Monument, PEGGY WAYBURN

Yukon Flats, WILBUR MILLS

The river seemed to tolerate us . . . it seemed a kindly yet reserved host—a giant of enormous power disposed to accept us and give us safe passage . . . We were interlopers, of course. This world belonged to the river, . . .
MARGARET A. MURIE
Two in the Far North

66

67   *Canadian Dogwood in Bloom*, PHILIP HYDE

Dall Sheep, G. C. KELLEY

Everything seemed so good, so in place, so appropriate, in this remote terrain, that it didn't even seem wrong when we discovered that the sheep had somehow sensed our coming and were more than a quarter of a mile away . . . when we got to the place where we expected to find them.
ROBERT MARSHALL, *Alaska Wilderness*

Beneath all those thriving blooms, all that Arctic beauty, is the solid frozen ground. In August autumn paints the blueberry bushes, cranberries, dwarf birch, and all other growth, and the landscape takes on the colors appropriate for that season.
OLAUS J. MURIE
Journeys to the Far North

Tundra Vista, WILBUR MILLS

Glacial Stream, WILBUR MILLS

70

We walked up the right shore among bare rocks intermingled with . . . bright lichen . . . No sight or sound or smell or feeling even remotely hinted of men or their creations. It seemed as if time had dropped away a million years and we were back in a primordial world. It was like discovering an unpeopled universe where only the laws of nature held sway.
ROBERT MARSHALL
Alaska Wilderness

Close at hand, only about ten miles air line to the north, was a precipitous pair of mountains, one on each side of the North Fork. I bestowed the name of Gates of the Arctic on them, christening the east portal Boreal Mountain and the west portal Frigid Crags.
ROBERT MARSHALL
Alaska Wilderness

71

Gates of the Arctic, WILBUR MILLS

Rainbow over Teklanika Rover, PHILIP HYDE

It was a sore temptation to follow . . . northward among the unexplored mountains stretching as far as we could see. However, that would have been a whole summer's journey, and we had only ten days left. So we classed that as a fine dream, unattainable as the end of the . . . rainbow in the canyon below us.
ROBERT MARSHALL
Alaska Wilderness

Mt. Blackburn, Wrangell Mountains, EDGAR WAYBURN

Lake Clark, EDGAR WAYBURN

We shall never understand the natural environment until we see it as a living organism. Land can be healthy or sick, fertile or barren, rich or poor, lovingly nurtured or bled white. Our present attitudes and laws governing the ownership and use of land represent an abuse of the concept of private property. Not so long ago our society permitted one human being to own another—to exploit him and even work him to death and not go to jail for it. This is no longer considered acceptable behavior, either by society or by the law. Yet in America today you can murder land for private profit. You can leave the corpse for all to see, and nobody calls the cops.
PAUL BROOKS
The Pursuit of Wilderness

On this day we sighted land in the direction of N. by W. and at a distance of about twenty-five German miles. This land consisted of huge, high, snow-covered mountains. We attempted to sail closer in towards land, but, as we had only light and shifting winds, it was not until 20th July that we drew near to it. At six o'clock in the evening of that day we let go our anchor in the neighbourhood of an island of considerable size, lying at no great distance from the mainland. (July 16, 1741)
SVEN WAXELL, *The Russian Expedition to America*

Tidal Flats, Katchemak Bay, PHILIP HYDE

Spring thaws bring breakup when melt waters loosen the ice and pressures fragment it into blocks and pieces, a process that fills the still, clear air with cannonades of sound.
PEGGY WAYBURN

Beaufort Sea, BERN KEATING

Mendenhall Glacier, PHILIP HYDE

It is then that the . . . bergs rise up from below—born of the depths. The enormous pressure to which their particles have been subjected for many centuries seems to have intensified their color. They have a pristine, elemental look. Their crystals have not seen the light since they fell in snowflakes back amid the mountains generations ago.
JOHN BURROUGHS
Harriman Alaska Expedition

It is an instructive example of a great glacier covering the hills and dales of a country that is not yet ready to be brought to the light of day—not only covering but creating a landscape with the features it is destined to have when, in the fullness of time, the fashioning ice-sheet shall be lifted by the sun, and the land become warm and fruitful.
JOHN MUIR, *Travels in Alaska*

77   *Columbia Glacier,* EDGAR WAYBURN

I was happy in the immediate presence of nature in its most staggering grandeur . . . so splendidly immense that all life seemed trivial in its presence. No doubt, too, there was the joy that here was something which mankind with all its mechanical power could not possibly hope to duplicate.
ROBERT MARSHALL, *Alaska Wilderness*

Below us was the great land. Indeed, all Glacier Bay is the great land, unique, wild, and magnificent. It should exist intact solely for its own sake. No justification, rationale, or excuse is needed. For its own sake and no other reason.
DAVE BOHN, *Glacier Bay, The Land and the Silence*

Johns Hopkins Inlet, Glacier Bay National Monument, PHILIP HYDE

Reflection Pond, Mt. McKinley, PHILIP HYDE

Polychrome Pass, PHILIP HYDE

Beaufort Lagoon, WILBUR MILLS

Summer Storm, WILBUR MILLS

Wolf, G. C. KELLEY

Humpback Whale, Glacier Bay, OLAF SOOT

Flying Squirrel, G. C. KELLEY

Bears in Tree, P. B. KAPLAN

I hope man has the vision to keep his civilization from at least a few such wildernesses as these—wilderness on the old, vast scale—so that wolf and caribou may continue to live as they always have; and for their own sake, not ours.
JOHN MILTON
*Nameless Valleys,
Shining Mountains*

Grizzly Bears, Arctic National Wildlife Range, EDGAR WAYBURN

Caribou, North Slope, WILBUR MILLS

We could see the sea-lions lift themselves up and gather in groups as the boat approached their rookery.

Then, after the landing was effected, they disappeared and . . . plunged into the water . . . the spectacle which the procession of the huge creatures made rushing across the beach to the sea was described as something most extraordinary. Those who were so fortunate as to witness it, placed it among the three or four most memorable events of their lives.

JOHN BURROUGHS
Harriman Alaska Expedition

Sea Lions, BOB AND IRA SPRING

Eskimos, King Island, BOB AND IRA SPRING

*The Alaskan Eskimos offer no threat to our way of
life. How far must we inevitably be a threat to
theirs?*
PAUL BROOKS, *The Pursuit of Wilderness*

*Because there are so few people in the Koyukuk,
the individual takes on a peculiar importance. . . .
Every individual . . . is important just because he is
alive, and . . . there is eliminated from his life all
the nerve-racking striving which accompanies any
effort to be distinguishable among the overwhelming numbers of the outside world.*
ROBERT MARSHALL, *Arctic Village*

Cabin, Wrangell Narrows, JAMES KOWALSKI

Eskimo Hunters, Point Barrow, BOB AND IRA SPRING

The Eskimo of Alaska . . . knows that he is the superior of anybody when it comes to living in the Arctic . . . We have learned so much from him and he is well aware of this. But there is this world-wide problem of . . . how to temper the impact of a highly technological, materialistic culture on a simpler culture . . . Simplicity of culture does not imply inferiority, although this is so often inferred when the simple culture crumbles under the weight of the complex.

F. Fraser Darling
Pelican in the Wilderness

Fishing Boats, Petersburg, JAMES KOWALSKI

Panting Bear Totem, TIM THOMPSON

If one inquires of an individual connected with the salmon industry in Alaska something about their numbers, he is at once told of the millions found there, and informed that the supply is inexhaustible. The same language will be used that was heard in past years with regard to the abundance of the wild pigeons, or of the buffalo, or of the fur-seals of Bering Sea. (1898)
GEORGE GRINNELL,
Harriman Alaska Expedition

Petersburg Harbor, JAMES KOWALSKI

Woodsman, P. B. KAPLAN

*"There's no law north
of the Arctic Circle.
Mustn't kill nobody;
mustn't steal;
to hell with the other laws."*
ROBERT MARSHALL, *Arctic Village*

*But the path began nowhere and ended
nowhere, and it remained mystery, as the
man who made it . . . remained mystery.*
JACK LONDON, *The Call of The Wild*

Abandoned Gold Mine, ED COOPER

Aspen, TIM THOMPSON

There is one word of advice and caution to be given those intending to visit Alaska for pleasure, for sight-seeing. If you are old, go by all means; but if you are young, wait. The scenery of Alaska is much grander than anything else of the kind in the world, and it is not well to dull one's capacity for enjoyment by seeing the finest first.
HENRY GANNETT
Harriman Alaska Expedition

98

Spruce Sentinels, WILBUR MILLS

This is part of the tundra's special attraction. First I am impressed by the space, the vastness, and the far mountains lining the horizon; then my eye is caught by the subtle shadings of brown and green, the delicate forms and contours of the nearly level landscape. Lastly, a bit of green moss . . . a flower . . . these hold my attention. You have to look at tundra this way, summing up the vast and the intimate.

JOHN MILTON, *Nameless Valleys, Shining Moutains*

Indian Burial Hut, TIM THOMPSON

Tundra Detail, PHILIP HYDE

I found most of the trees fairly loaded with mosses. Some broadly palmated branches had beds of yellow moss so wide and deep that when they were wet they must weigh a hundred pounds or even more. Upon these moss-beds ferns and grasses and even good-sized seedling trees grow, making beautiful hanging gardens in which the curious spectacle is presented of old trees holding . . . their own children in their arms, nourished by rain and dew and the decaying leaves showered down to them by their parents. The branches upon which these beds of mossy soil rest become flat and irregular like weathered roots or the antlers of deer, and at length die; and when the whole tree has thus been killed it seems to be standing on its head with roots in the air.
JOHN MUIR, *Travels in Alaska*

Rain Forest, Bartlett Cove, TIM THOMPSON

Marsh, Tongass National Forest, PHILIP HYDE

Maps

Alaska is immense. Its 586,000 square miles cover an area nearly one-fifth the size of the contiguous forty-eight States of the Union, sprawling across about 21 degrees of latitude and 43 degrees of longitude. If Alaska's southernmost tip could be placed on the mouth of the Savannah River, and its northernmost point on Lake of the Woods, Minnesota, the Aleutian Islands would stretch west of Los Angeles.

Within Alaska the North American continent reaches its highest point in Mt. McKinley (altitude 20,300 feet), as well as its lowest in the Aleutian Trench (25,000 feet below sea level). There are hundreds of volcanoes, thousands of glaciers, numerous great rivers, countless lakes, and some 35,000 miles of coast. The range of climate and precipitation is as impressive as the landscape.

The public lands of Alaska are presently and finally being disposed of. The maps on the following pages illustrate some of Alaska's extraordinary physiographic features, the pattern of its proposed subdivisions, and conversationists' proposal of areas which must be protected if Alaska's great land and the life it supports are to survive.

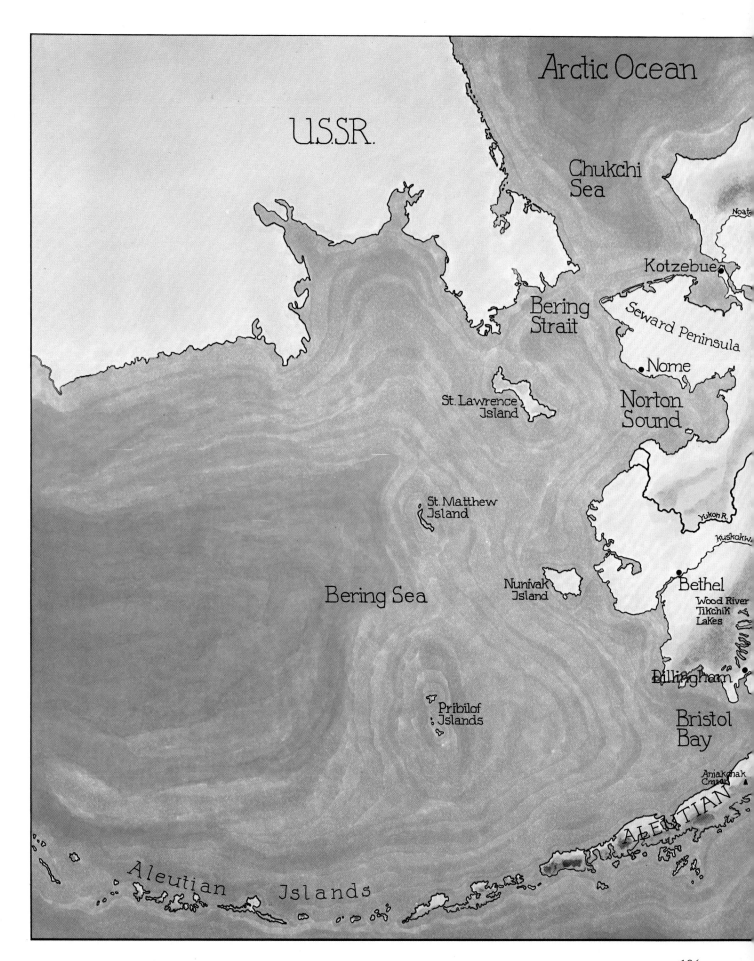

Arctic Ocean

U.S.S.R.

Chukchi
Sea

Noata

Kotzebue

Bering
Strait

Seward Peninsula

Nome

St. Lawrence
Island

Norton
Sound

St. Matthew
Island

Yukon R.

Kuskokw.

Nunivak
Island

Bethel

Wood River
Tikchik
Lakes

Bering Sea

Dillingham

Pribilof
Islands

Bristol
Bay

Aniakchak
Crater

ALEUTIAN

Aleutian   Islands

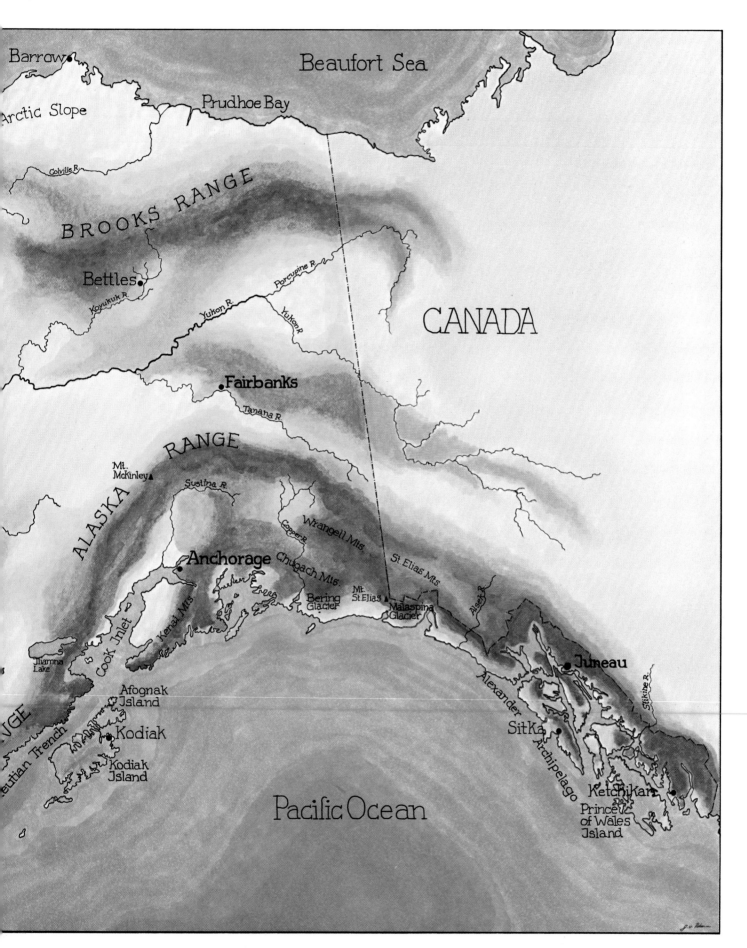

Barrow

Beaufort Sea

Arctic Slope

Prudhoe Bay

Colville R.

BROOKS RANGE

Bettles

Koyukuk R.

Porcupine R.

CANADA

Yukon R.

Yukon R.

Fairbanks

Tanana R.

RANGE

Mt. McKinley▲

Susitna R.

ALASKA

Wrangell Mts.

Copper R.

Anchorage

Chugach Mts.

St. Elias Mts.

Bering Glacier

Mt. St. Elias▲

Malaspina Glacier

Alsek R.

Kenai Mts.

Cook Inlet

Juneau

Iliamna Lake

Alexander

Stikine R.

Afognak Island

NGE

Sitka

Archipelago

eutian Trench

Kodiak

Kodiak Island

Ketchikan

Prince of Wales Island

Pacific Ocean

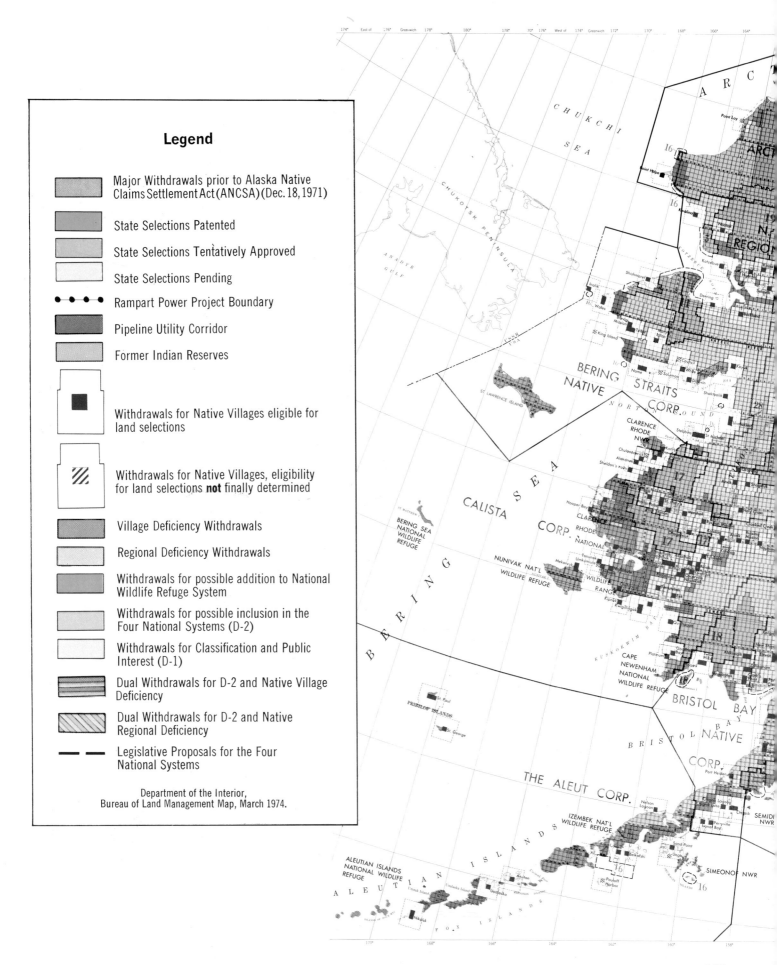

Legend

Major Withdrawals prior to Alaska Native Claims Settlement Act (ANCSA) (Dec. 18, 1971)

State Selections Patented

State Selections Tentatively Approved

State Selections Pending

Rampart Power Project Boundary

Pipeline Utility Corridor

Former Indian Reserves

Withdrawals for Native Villages eligible for land selections

Withdrawals for Native Villages, eligibility for land selections **not** finally determined

Village Deficiency Withdrawals

Regional Deficiency Withdrawals

Withdrawals for possible addition to National Wildlife Refuge System

Withdrawals for possible inclusion in the Four National Systems (D-2)

Withdrawals for Classification and Public Interest (D-1)

Dual Withdrawals for D-2 and Native Village Deficiency

Dual Withdrawals for D-2 and Native Regional Deficiency

Legislative Proposals for the Four National Systems

Department of the Interior,
Bureau of Land Management Map, March 1974.

108

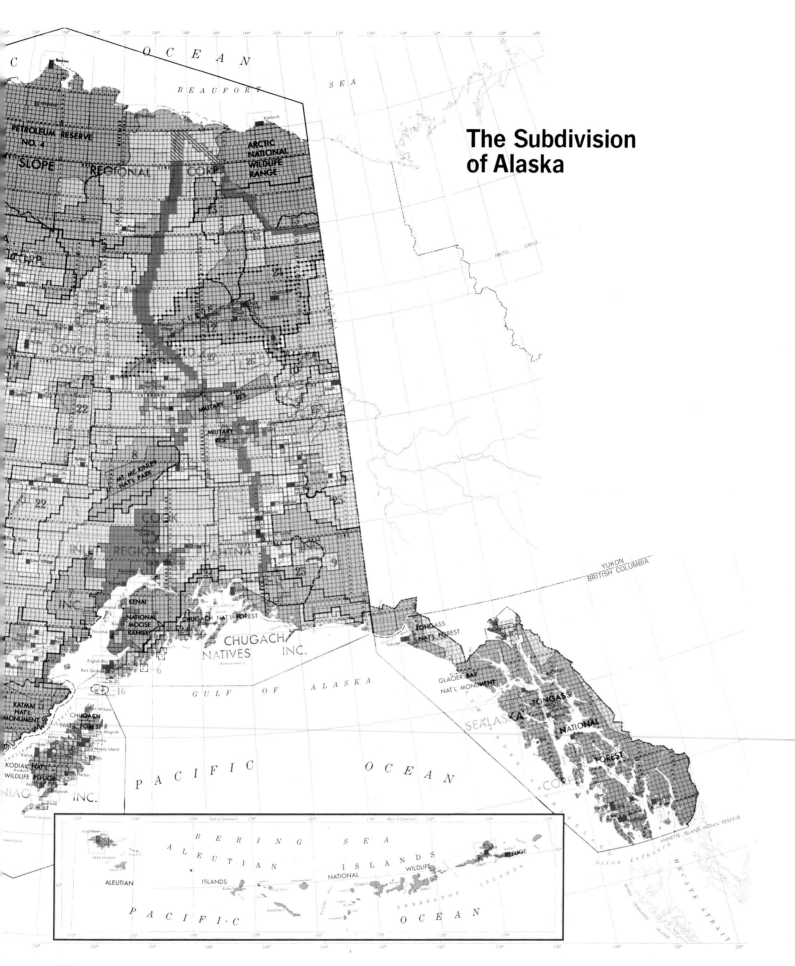

The Subdivision
of Alaska

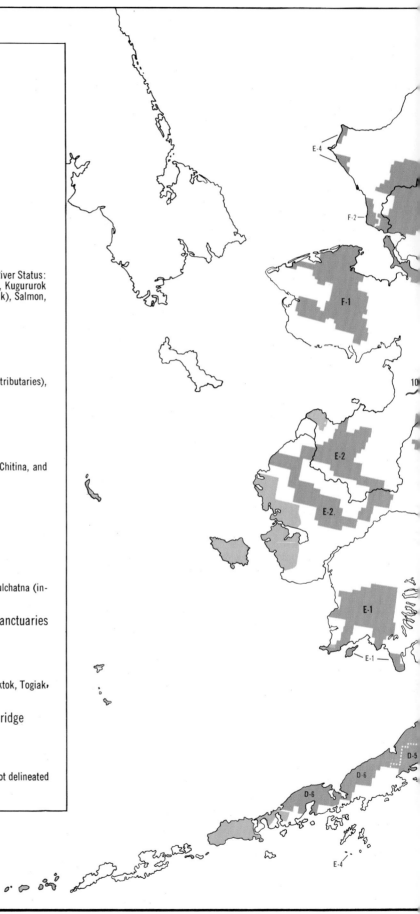

Legend

 Existing National Forests, Parks, and Wildlife Refuge Systems

 Pipeline Utility Corridor and Withdrawals for utility corridor

 The National Interest Lands
(See pp. 138–150 for detailed descriptions.)

Area A: The Arctic and Sub-Arctic

Unit A-1: Gates of the Arctic National Park
Unit A-2: Noatak National Ecological Reserve
Unit A-3: Kobuk Valley National Monument
Unit A-4: Selawik National Wildlife Range

The following rivers, in part or in whole, are proposed for Wild River Status: the Alatna, Killik, Kobuk, Noatak (including the Cutler, Aniuk, Kugururok and Kelly), North Fork of the Koyukuk (including the Tinayguk), Salmon, Squirrel, and Wind*

Area B: The Arctic-Interior Ecosystem

Unit B-1: Arctic National Wildlife Range
Unit B-2: Yukon Flats National Wildlife Range
Unit B-3: Yukon-Charley Rivers National Park

Rivers proposed for Wild River Status: the Black (including all tributaries), Beaver Creek, Charley, Ivishak, Porcupine, and Sheenjek*

Area C: South Central-Southeast Alaska

Unit C-1: Wrangell-Kluane International Park
Unit C-2: National Forest Additions
Unit C-3: Kenai Fjords National Monument

Rivers proposed for Wild River Status: the Alsek, Bremner, Chitina, and Copper*

Area D: The Alaska Range-Aleutian Chain

Unit D-1: Mt. McKinley National Park
Unit D-2: Lake Clark National Park
Unit D-3: Iliamna National Wildlife Range
Unit D-4: Katmai National Park
Unit D-5: Aniakchak Caldera National Monument
Unit D-6: Alaska Peninsula National Brown Bear Range

Rivers proposed for Wild River Status: the Aniakchak and Mulchatna (including Chilikadrotna)*

Area E: Western and Central Alaska—Migratory Bird Sanctuaries

Unit E-1: Togiak National Wildlife Range
Unit E-2: Yukon Delta National Wildlife Range
Unit E-3: Koyukuk National Wildlife Range
Unit E-4: Coastal National Wildlife Refuge

Rivers proposed for Wild River Status: the Andreafsky, Kanektok, Togiak, and Nowitna*

Area F: Northwest Alaska: Lands of the Bering Sea Bridge

Unit F-1: Chukchi-Imuruk National Ecological Reserve
Unit F-2: Cape Krusenstern National Monument

Rivers proposed for Wild River Status: the Kuzitrin*

*Proposed Wild Rivers within National Interest Areas are not delineated on this map. See text, page 149 for details.

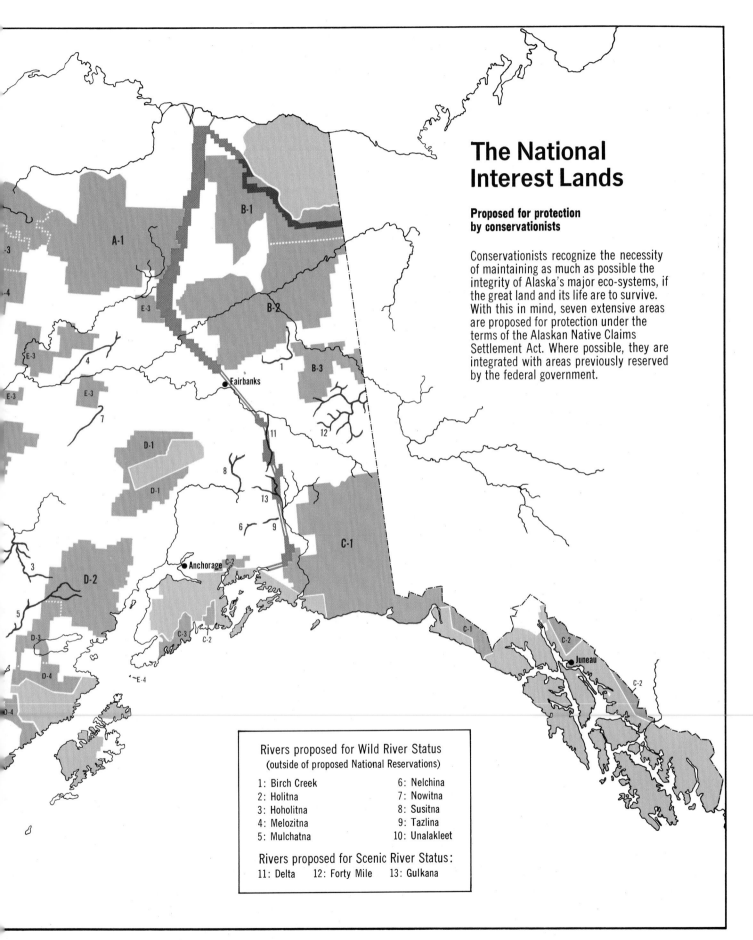

The National Interest Lands

Proposed for protection by conservationists

Conservationists recognize the necessity of maintaining as much as possible the integrity of Alaska's major eco-systems, if the great land and its life are to survive. With this in mind, seven extensive areas are proposed for protection under the terms of the Alaskan Native Claims Settlement Act. Where possible, they are integrated with areas previously reserved by the federal government.

Rivers proposed for Wild River Status
(outside of proposed National Reservations)

1: Birch Creek	6: Nelchina
2: Holitna	7: Nowitna
3: Hoholitna	8: Susitna
4: Melozitna	9: Tazlina
5: Mulchatna	10: Unalakleet

Rivers proposed for Scenic River Status:
11: Delta   12: Forty Mile   13: Gulkana

3. The Last True Wilderness

PEGGY WAYBURN

Never before this had I been embosomed in
scenery so hopelessly beyond description.

JOHN MUIR, *Travels in Alaska*

It has always been difficult to describe Alaska, to convey its prodigious scale, variety, and vigor, as well as its overwhelming beauty. There is the simple matter of its size: Alaska's 365 million acres sprawl over roughly 21 degrees of latitude, 43 degrees of longitude (if the Aleutian chain is included), and to add another dimension, four time zones. To see all of Alaska—let alone become well acquainted with it—would require viewing over 1 million acres every day for a full year. To explore all of its 34,000-mile coast, which makes Alaska one of the world's largest peninsulas, would demand examining some 94 miles of shoreline each day throughout another year-long expedition. In the words of the explorer Alfred Hulse Brooks, the territory of Alaska is truly of "continental magnitude."

The relief of the Alaskan terrain is as awesome as its immensity. About a third of Alaska's land is relatively flat and situated at fairly low elevations. Across this gently tilted country even the greatest rivers are compelled to slow down and loop in huge meanders, unwinding their broad sinuous pathways through tundra and muskeg, where in the summer thousands of thaw lakes gleam in the perpetual sun. The rest of Alaska is mountains—from low, rolling foothills to sky-filling, thunderous, and snow-shining mountains. For in Alaska the land of North America surges to its greatest and perhaps most spectacular heights in the culmination of two great mountain systems. With the plateau between them, these mountain systems form a major physiographic feature of the continent. Through the southern parts of the state the Pacific Mountain System curves broadly in a double crescent of wildly tumultuous land. In the north of the state, roughly delineating the Arctic Circle which it embraces, the Rocky Mountain System sweeps in from Canada to form the Brooks Range. In between lies the Intermontane Plateau which itself has mountainous regions, though not on so grand a scale.

(Adding another, though unseen, dimension to the Alaskan terrain, some of earth's most impressive seismic zones cleave its land mass to enormous depths. The Chatham trough slumps 2,900 feet while the Aleutian Trench sags 25,000 feet below sea level. Thus in Alaska the continent not only soars to its highest but dips to its lowest point. The difference between these two extremes of Alaskan land is over 45,000 feet, nearly nine vertical miles.)

The southernmost crescent or massive ridge of the Pacific Mountain System includes parts of the Coastal Range and the Pacific Border Range. These ranges are so vast that each contains several respectable—and gorgeous—mountain systems, the Kenai and Chugach

Mountains, the St. Elias and Fairweather Mountains, and the Chilkat-Baranof Mountains among them. Many of these mountains thrust their peaks into the clouds two and three miles above sea level. A few soar from 18,000 to 20,000 feet. The summit ridges of most of them are buried deep in snow and ice fields, but some have dark jagged arêtes so sheer that they cannot hold the snow.

In Alaska's southeast region, the walls of these mountains lift up almost directly from the sea, forming an unbelievably high shimmering white barrier against the horizon. On a "blue day" they make an extravagant backdrop for the lush evergreen forests that rim the shore. Spread at the feet of these mountains are immense fans of glaciers thickly striped and stenciled with ridges of dark earth, each of which marks the ice of a separate watershed.

In the massive northern ridge of the Pacific Mountain System lie the Aleutian and Alaska Ranges, both of which also contain numerous spectacular mountain systems. Among the Aleutian mountains are a number of earth's major volcanoes. Some, like Mt. Veniaminof and Mt. Aniakchak, are of staggering mass; the former—named for a man who himself was a giant among his peers—is over 8,000 feet high, has a 600-square-mile base and a 25-square-mile crater.

The Alaska Range crests in Mt. McKinley, at 20,320 feet the highest mountain on the North American continent. Flanking this titan, called Denali, the Great One, by earlier, more poetic people, are other mountains that are titans in their own rights. The peaks of the Alaska Range, like those further south, are perpetually sheathed in snow and ice. Against skies which often brood dark with storms, they gleam like burnished pewter. In their high amphitheaters lie immense glaciers veined with blue crevasses. Down their steep slopes ice falls move slowly, while avalanches of looser snow cascade in glittering streams. Their foothills, which may be nearly mile-high themselves, are more gently rounded, often snow-free in summer, and streaked in unexpectedly bright and beautiful patterns, inspiring such a place-name as Polychrome Pass in the heart of Mt. McKinley National Park.

Between the great ridges of the Pacific Mountain System lies the depression in the earth's crust known as the Coastal Trough province. In the midst of its lowland areas and rolling uplands shaped by long-gone glaciers there are several mountain ranges, one of which—the Wrangells—is among Alaska's mightiest. This oval group of massive volcanoes has six peaks over 12,000 feet and climaxes in Mt. Blackburn, over 16,500 feet high. These snowy mountains have rugged cliffs and castellated ridges jutting above the many glaciers that are born and nourished in the cradles of their high cirques. Huge ice rivers scrape their slow way between the sharp ridges, merging at last into one vast glacier, the Bering, the longest in North America. There are canyons here deep and spacious enough to hold Yosemite Valley with room to spare. Slender waterfalls plume and sway from the hanging valleys. Glacial rivers pour their turbid racing waters between teardrop bars and islands of polished gravel. To some people this is the most magnificent country in Alaska, but like any judgment of Alaskan scenery, this must be arbitrary.

There is active volcanism in the Wrangell Mountains and the Alaska Range as well as in the Aleutians. Taken together, Alaska's snow-streaked volcanoes form the northern segment of the great "Circle of Fire," the ring of active craters that rims the Pacific Ocean. One of these volcanoes, Novarupta, near Mt. Katmai, put on an impressive display in 1912, drowning hundreds of miles around it in incandescent ash and spewing an estimated four-fifths of a cubic mile of volcanic dust into the sky to rain down onto the earth for five years thereafter. The region around it, called the Valley of Ten Thousand Smokes because of the innumerable steam vents that formed in the layer of ash, was declared a National Monument by President Woodrow Wilson in 1918. With later addition, this has turned out to be the single largest land unit presently in the National Park system.

Through much of the Pacific Mountain System active mountain building is in progress, with the earth's crust moving restlessly as it did in so spectacular a manner on Good Friday in 1964 in the Chugach Mountains and the Gulf of Alaska. It is hard to convey the magnitude of an earthquake like this one, which at 8.4 on the Richter scale was among the greatest registered in modern times. Whole blocks of houses in Anchorage were swallowed by the earth; parts of Valdez slid into the sea. In places the ocean floor sank, in others it lifted to form new land. Giant tsunamis—mistakenly called tidal waves—overwhelmed the Pacific shoreline as far south as California. Some river banks pulled apart and collapsed the bridges spanning them; others shoved together and bent railroad tracks crossing them as though they were picture wire. For eight hours after the initial shocks the ground level of waters in Alaska fluctuated wildly, as much as twenty-four feet. Water levels elsewhere on the continent responded to this massive shudder of the planet as well—in swimming pools in Texas, in reservoirs in Michigan, and in wells in South Dakota. Even wells in Puerto Rico and Australia rose and sank as much as three-and-one-half feet. This was literally an earth-shaking event, and on a global scale.

Alaska's spectacular earthquakes and volcanism result from its active geologic condition. According to recent theories, the southern arc of the Alaskan coast, lapped by the Pacific Ocean, marks the junction of massive tectonic plates—huge pieces of the earth's crust—which are interacting constantly. These plates of crustal land float on the earth's molten core like giant rafts on a fiery sea. Moved by forces not yet entirely understood, certain plates are pulled inexorably beneath others. Thus the floor of the Pacific Ocean is being thrust slowly but surely beneath the Alaskan land mass, shoving up the earth into towering walls of mountains along the line of collision. Where the crust is broken and torn by such collision, the hot magma may well up, as it does frequently in Alaska's volcanoes. The southern Alaskan terrain fits current geological ideas so perfectly that it is often used as a classic example.

Accompanying the continuous mountain building and volcanism in Alaska, there is widespread fracturing, or rifting, of the land. Thus a beautiful network of fault lines laces through the Pacific Mountain System, delineating the uneasy sections of the earth. In terms of geologic time, no part of this mountainous terrain can remain completely stable for very long.

The spur of the Rockies that forms Alaska's Brooks Range is different in character. In Paleozoic times this region was the floor of a vast, warm, shallow sea—a catch basin for the endless drift of marine materials. During the eons these sediments were compacted into layer upon layer of rock. Now uplifted, bent, twisted, sometimes baked by earth's fierce, deep heat, these sedimentary rocks occur as limestone, sandstone, shale, schist, and slate, interlaced with quartzite, and colored soft grays, blues, browns, pale golds, and creamy whites. In places folded into great curves and arches, in others upthrust at sharp angles in even strata, these rocks seem to soar out of the ground in masses that may reach 6,000 to 9,000 feet.

In the middle of the Brooks Range rugged younger granite intrusions thrust up a cluster of stunning peaks, their summits deeply incised and serrated into needles and spires, their flanks smoothed and polished by glaciers. These, the Arregitch Peaks, are a rock climber's paradise. To their east, occasional outpourings of dark igneous rock have formed mountains that stand in somber contrast, like Doonerak, the huge forbidding "devil" mountain named and beloved by Robert Marshall, one of the region's earliest and most eloquent advocates. Nearby, Mt. Boreal and Frigid Crags, and the Gates of the Arctic, also named by Marshall, flank the clear, bright waters of the North Fork of the Koyukuk River and form a grand portal to the land beyond. And lying at the head of the large valleys on both the north and south sides of the Brooks Range, resting in depressions scooped out by earlier glaciers, are some of Alaska's loveliest blue lakes.

Although this entire region once bore a heavy burden of snow and ice, only remnants of the once-great glaciers remain. Hanging glaciers still cling to some of the high cirques, their melt waters plummeting over the steep cliffs in spectacular waterfalls. Patches of ice and snow spot and streak the higher rocks in startling patterns. A dusting of white may be left on the peaks during an August storm, but most of this area is free of snow in summer. The ice fields of the Pacific Mountain System are absent. This is more intimate country, older, more open, more softened by time. Its green swards of tundra are easy to travel in many places. And to some people this scenery surpasses any other in Alaska, again an arbitrary choice.

To the north of the Brooks Range lie rolling foothills and undulating plateaus which end in places in a low, abrupt scarp. Tilting very gently from this scarp is the Arctic Coastal Plain, an extension of the vast Central Plains Region of the lower continent. This broad apron of land, commonly called the North Slope, slips beneath the Arctic Ocean in such a barely perceptible gradient that its coastline makes little dent in the landscape. The shore, which may be only one or two feet high, cannot be seen in places from a mile or so at sea.

Gathering the waters from Alaska's mountains is a spectacular network of wild rivers. Almost all of those rising in the Pacific Mountain System are swift glacial streams which pour from the snow and ice fields that drape its peaks. These rivers pile up into deep torrents as they cut their way between steep canyon walls. But on the flatlands they braid out into interlacing channels which may sprawl as much as a mile wide. One channel is always the deepest and therefore the principal pathway of the river, but even an expert canoeist or kayaker may be challenged to find it in the broad web of milky waters.

The Alaskan rivers that rise in unglaciated watersheds—as do many of those in the inland regions—can run as clear as glass. They may curl in broad, blue-green ribbons across the flat plateaus or surge tea-colored, stained by the bog and muskeg through which they pass. A good strong summer storm can swell the flow of any Alaskan river in a spectacular manner. The muddied foam-streaked waters can rise four or five feet overnight flooding the low-lying banks, drowning the mouths of tributaries, and incidentally drenching or even dislodging an unwary traveler camped on a river bar.

Alaska's principal rivers—the Kuskokwim, the Copper, the Kobuk, the Porcupine, Noatak, Susitna, Stikine, Nushagak—the list is long—are major waterways by any standards. Those which drain into the sea, such as the Copper, Alsek, Stikine, Taku, Noatak, Colville and Sagavanirktok, form immense estuarine areas along the coast. Almost all of those which drain inland, however, feed the most fabulous river of all, the Yukon. Rising in Canada, it takes water from the Brooks Range and the Pacific Mountain systems and most of the mountains in between. Swinging 1,400 miles through Alaska's Intermontane Plateau, it is one of the greatest waterways of the continent. Nearly joining the Kuskokwim before emptying into the Bering Sea, it forms with that river a delta that spreads over 26,000 square miles, one of the world's finest wetlands. The salmon that spawn at the headwaters of the Yukon must not only thread their way through an incredible maze of stream channels which lace this delta, but also make their way 2,000 miles up the swollen, muddy waters of their ancestral river until they find the place of their birth. And for men, as well as for fish, this extraordinary river is navigable all the way.

Despite persistent legend, Alaska is obviously not a land of endless and everlasting ice and snow. It has, in fact, a number of distinct climates. Indeed, in this vast territory the overall temperatures and amounts of precipitation match the geography in scale and variety.

Southeast Alaska is one of the wettest, lushest areas on the North American continent. January temperatures along the coast hover around the freezing mark. The Pacific Ocean washes its warm currents into the Gulf of Alaska and the Inside Passage and moisture-laden winds (some spawned in the Aleutians) encounter the towering mountain wall along the shore. The resultant precipatation is spectacular—an average of 220 inches a year drenches parts of Baranof Island. The state's capital, Juneau, with a winter climate similar to that of Chicago, gets soaked with nearly 90 inches annually. Whittier, tucked into the mountains that cradle Prince William Sound, gathers 120 inches. At higher altitudes the rain freezes and continuously lavishes the vast glacial systems of the Pacific Mountain system with new snow and ice.

North of the Pacific Coastal area the picture changes abruptly. Much of the area has a "frost climate": temperatures fluctuate widely with the annual average generally below freezing. The land is subject to alternate freezing and thawing—powerful processes of geologic change. And like the temperature, the precipitation plummets.

On the Arctic Coastal plain the rainfall is scant, an average of about four inches a year at

Point Barrow, which is only 1,250 miles from the North Pole. However, the influence of the Arctic Ocean—like that of all the ocean waters which rim Alaska—is considerable, and even here the summer days can be mild, with the thermometer in the 50s and 60s and occasionally the 70s. But the winters are bitter, with minus 50-degree temperatures and cruel, relentless winds that drive the snow like sandblasting machines. Cold locks the land, the shallow sea, the tens of thousands of thaw lakes, and even the rivers—which freeze to their beds—in a solid grip of ice. Spring thaws bring "break up," when melt waters loosen the ice and pressures fragment it into blocks and pieces, a process that fills the still, clear air with cannonades of sound.

In the interior of Alaska the moderating influence of the oceans is missing, rainfall is light, and the extremes of temperature are phenomenal. In summer, the people of Fairbanks, the state's second largest city and home of the University of Alaska, may swelter in 90 or even 100 degree heatwaves. In turn, the winters are among the coldest on the North American continent. With the thermometer at minus 60 to 75 degrees, even the smog freezes (a serious health hazard), and parking meters must have electric outlets for plugging in heaters to keep car engines thawed.

Two interesting phenomena are associated with Alaska's climatic conditions; one is the persistence of its glaciers, among the most extensive and magnificent remaining anywhere on earth. (Only the glacial systems of Greenland and the Antarctic are larger.) The other is the presence of permafrost, which may be considered a kind of underground glacier itself, being a condition in which the moisture in the soil and the soil itself are perpetually frozen—sometimes for thousands of years. (There is actually such a thing as "dry" permafrost, in which no moisture is present and the soil alone is frozen, but this is uncommon in Alaska, where one of the most outstanding characteristics of the landscape is its wetness, be it frozen or thawed.) These two phenomena are constantly working over the Alaskan earth, arranging and rearranging it.

Glaciers are great architects of the land. They quarry, polish, and sculpture the earth, grinding up bedrock, fracturing and scraping off pieces of rock, and freighting them great distances as they slowly move. Piling up clutters of gravel, grit, and boulders, glaciers can create a number of new features on a landscape—mounds, hills, and extensive ridges. They can also plow out deep troughs or plaster the ground with fine silt and completely alter the topography. And glaciers are constantly determining where new lakes will lie. They hollow out bedrock to act as a catch basin when their ice melts. They heap up dams to hold new tarns and ponds. They even plug the exit of their own melt water to gather pools of milky, turquoise water, which may empty out in spectacular fashion. Glaciers also spawn great rivers, which themselves are powerful agents of geological change, incising the land as they plunge to the sea, carrying with them the grains of mountains, hills, and flatlands—all the terrain through which they travel.

Permafrost is an equally effective, though less understood, geologic agent which models the landscape wherever it exists. Away from the Pacific coastal areas of Alaska it is widespread. Permafrost underlies the entire land area of the North Slope in a huge slab of frozen ground at least 1,000 feet thick, which rests from 6 inches to 4 feet below the surface soil. South of the Arctic Circle the permafrost is still widespread, although it becomes discontinuous and then patchy in the lower latitudes, occuring in heavily shaded places, on the northern slope of hills, and in smaller and less dense shields. Anchorage, where most of the population of Alaska is centered, lies just outside the area of permafrost. Only a few miles to the north, however, farmers of the Matanuska Valley, Alaska's celebrated farming region, may have to contend with this unique condition of the land, which can make a nightmare out of traditional agricultural practices.

Permafrost and the skin of surface soil that covers it are so closely interdependent that the two cannot be considered separately. They interact with one another in a condition of delicate balance which, if disturbed, can destroy them both. The skin that covers an area of permafrost may be a thin layer of debris—formed for example, by the alternate freezing, shattering, and thawing of a rocky area—or it may be a thicker skin of tundra or muskeg, that is, topsoil built up over a longer period of time. Although this skin of debris, tundra, or muskeg will freeze and thaw with the changing seasons, it more or less permanently insulates the ground beneath it and keeps it continuously frozen. The permafrost area, in turn, stays as firm as a block of cement as long as it is insulated, performing the function of solid bedrock.

On slopes with a core of permafrost, freezing and thawing loosen the surface soil, causing it to "creep" slowly, and gravity pulls it gently down the hill. When saturated thoroughly, surface soils in such a situation turn to a thick sludge in spring thaws and flow more readily in a motion described as "solifluction." On steep slopes underlain with permafrost the surface soil is apt to be highly unstable, and landslides are frequent in warm weather.

Both creep and solifluction move the surface layer of soil in characteristic ways, forming recognizable features on the landscape, such as solifluction lobes. In ways still not entirely understood, these processes—linked so closely to the alternate freezing and thawing of the terrain—result in the sorting out of soil materials along with their rearrangement. Thus, networks of small polygons may be formed, with the finer silt in the soil being mounded in the center, while the coarser particles form the perimeters. Much larger polygons are formed in tundra areas by ice wedges and make a characteristic ground pattern over tens of thousands of miles. Pingos, large blisters of ice which may push up the turf into rounded or cone-shaped hummocks as high as 100 feet, are common features of the frozen North Slope.

On gently sloping lowlands and flatlands, areas of permafrost act as pans beneath the surface tundra and muskeg. The solidly frozen ground prevents water from percolating through the surface and keeps the tundra and muskeg saturated, a condition necessary for its survival. Thus, it is permafrost that accounts for the sloshy muskegs and tundras of much of Alaska in the summer. These vast swampy areas which form in warm weather are formidable barriers to foot travel, being better suited to a moose's big splayed hoof than to a human's more spindly equipment. And such wet areas are heaven for mosquitos and other winged insects.

When the skin of surface soil is ripped off an area of permafrost, an inexorable chain of events is set into motion, the process of Arctic erosion. Exposed permafrost, bare of its insulation, loses its solid bedrock qualities. In summer it thaws, collapses on itself, and forms a pit or ditch of icy soup or mush, which gradually becomes a tarn. Alternative freezing and thawing cause the banks to fall in and the area, called a thermokarst, grows ever larger. If mutilation of a permafrost area is caused by the running of seismic lines, the cutting of raw roads, or the incision of tractor wheels, extensive canals may ensue—waterways that grow ever wider.

Permafrost has always posed challenging problems for builders of any structure that penetrates or disturbs the ground. The innocent homesteader, for example, who dug a cellar for his house and installed a furnace was in for a surprise; when winter came and he stoked up his fire, his house was apt to collapse as the ground beneath it melted. Even without a cellar, any house built on permafrost will shift around sooner or later, its floors will arc up, its doors jam, and its walls cant at drunken angles as the ground beneath it buckles and heaves. Some public buildings constructed recently in permafrost country have had freezer systems built into their foundations to keep them upright during summer thaws; others are rooted to great depths with steel beams.

Sewer lines laid through regions of permafrost may not last out a season, and septic tanks are hopelessly impractical. Roads sliced through permafrost are not only a challenge to build but enormously costly to maintain. Permafrost action can crack concrete as though it were an eggshell. It can also realign railroad ties, and thrust up poles or piers sunk into it as though they were match sticks. Farming in a region of permafrost can be an experiment in hydroponics during summer months, and thermokarsts have been known to swallow the bulldozers of unsuspecting farmers.

It is Alaska's location on the planet that is responsible for its remarkable climatic conditions. Lying in the northern latitudes, Alaska never gets a full, hot flood of sunshine. (The resultant relatively small amount of evaporation, incidentally, accounts in part for its perennial wetness.) And while its seasons hinge basically on the equinox and solstice, as do seasons everywhere on earth, Alaska's situation gives a unique rhythm to its periods of daylight and darkness. Here in "the land of the midnight sun" the skies never become entirely dark—even in the southeast—from May 10 to August 2. For weeks the pale night skies are starless, with the moon being the only nocturnal heavenly body to occupy their transparent depths. From November 18 through January 24 north of the Arctic Circle the sun gets over the horizon barely or not at all, and the sky teems perpetually with stars—although their light may be drowned in the brilliance of the frequent auroras. On a December day in Juneau, the street lights are off for only five hours; in Anchorage it's more likely four. Thus, Alaska gets its daylight and darkness in long, heavy doses, almost as though its year were one great long day and night. It is at high noon of that day—during the brief span of summer months—that all living things, including humans, come wide awake and intensely cram their activities into the short, sweet period of sunlight.

Other phenomena are associated with Alaska's location on the planet. There is the quality of its light. The higher the latitude, the lower the angle of the sun and the longer its rays must travel before they touch the land. Thus, on the North Slope the light is dilute; the sky seems paler and the color of the landscape appears faded, as though stroked in soft pastels. Although the light in Anchorage is more intense, the people living there may blink hard at the brilliance of the colors in, say, Reno, finding them as vivid as neon compared to those at home. In southeast Alaska the sun spills its light more heavily and the skies glow a deeper, more vibrant blue, which floats over the glossy waters of the bays and inlets of the Inside Passage, making for the "blue days" prized by natives and tourists alike.

But even in the southeast the sun never passes directly overhead. Everywhere in Alaska the sunshine slants in more or less horizontally, backlighting objects on the landscape and giving them perpetual shadows. Thus, seen from the air, the sparse black spruce trees of the taiga forest appear to be multiple gnomons—or indicators—on a vast, improbable sundial of tundra. Their individual shadows lie parallel, penciling the landscape with straight stripes that shift with the shifting sun.

Alaska, the Great Land, an early people named it because this simple title seemed to articulate best this country's remarkable nature—its vastness and its heady extremes of topography, climate, and light and darkness. Yet another major aspect of Alaska's greatness is its extraordinary vitality. While change is one of earth's necessary and universal processes, it seems to occur more slowly in many other places on the planet; the Alaskan land is alive with change. It is being continuously worked over by glaciers, chiseled by rivers, beaten and drenched by storms, shattered and remodeled by alternate freezing and thawing, showered with incandescent dust, and jarred and upthrust in massive earthquakes. The Alaskan peninsula is one of the most dynamic land masses on earth. And its vigor adds an intensity to its times of quietness: there is a purity and serenity in Alaska's clear blue summer days that is not to be found in more placid places.

Another part of Alaska's enormous vitality rests in the fabric of life which has enmeshed itself into its land and water and air. The Arctic and sub-Arctic environments plainly pose some particular, and formidable, requirements for living things. Life must be tough, strong, ingenious, and resilient to survive. And life is: it may be marginal, or prodigiously successful, but it is everywhere and in unexpected variety in Alaska.

This life may take the small, elegant form of a tundra flower, or the powerful shape of a glacier bear. It may be seen in the beating wings of sandhill cranes in urgent flight through the pale evening skies of September, or in the bright surge of salmon up a clear, singing stream. It may be heard in the raucous call of a Steller's jay, or in the voice of the wolf, spokesman of the wilderness. It may be marveled at in the seed of a lupine, viable after being sealed for thousands of years in the frozen ground. It has many strands, Alaska's web of life, and some are tenuous.

119

It has taken eons to weave itself with delicacy and precision into a dynamic, demanding environment, and to achieve a perfect, though fragile, interdependence and balance.

The most essential threads of this living fabric—indeed its very warp—are, of course, the green plants, which alone can capture the energy of the sun and make it available to other forms of life. Several different plant communities are knit tightly into the Alaskan land; perhaps the most distinctive is that of the tundra. The tundra is so extensive and complex that it is considered one of earth's seven biomes, or major living communities.

In broad differentiation there are four types of tundra in Alaska—the heath, tussock, alpine, and wet sedge or meadow. Together, they cover enormous reaches of the Alaskan land. Tundra clothes much of the seemingly barren Aleutian Island chain, the high, windy slopes of Alaska's mountains, the rolling foothills and plains of the north and the taiga of the interior. The tundra community may appear at first glance to be not just unspectacular, but monotonous. A swath of alpine tundra, for instance, may stretch for miles, a dull gray-green, which looks as bleak as a desert in mid-summer. Yet a closer view reveals that it is napped like deep velvet with a marvelous assortment of miniature plants.

One of the most important of the tundra plants is the lichen, which comprises on an average about a third of the tundra community. The lichen grows over the cold, sparse topsoil, builds up the soil and at the same time holds it in place. Looking like a softly curling papery gray moss, "reindeer" lichen covers vast areas with its furze. The many varieties of lichens are among the toughest pioneer plants, finding a toehold in the harshest, coldest places. Indeed, lichens may be the only living things a climber finds on a high Alaskan summit. (This hardy little plant is made up, in fact, of two different plant species, a green alga and a fungus, which coexist symbiotically, the fungus providing the home, the alga making the food.) But despite its toughness, the lichen of the tundra may take as long as forty years to establish itself.

Along with the lichen, there is embroidered into the Arctic tundra a whole garden of dwarf flowering plants and tiny shrubs that live briefly and gloriously in the summer, leafing, flowering and fruiting, crowding the duties of a lifetime into the short season of steady sunshine. Inches-high dogwood stars the tundra ground with its flat, creamy-white blossoms. The heather's blooms hang like small white bells. Miniature willows bear usual-size catkins, which seem absurdly large on their short branches. Tiny birch and poplars tremble their leaves in the summer breezes. A whole spectrum of berrying plants, including the most succulent of blueberries, dot the tundra with their tempting fruit. When the cool days of August come, the leaves of the flowering plants begin to turn every shade of rose and red and crimson. The small birches, poplars, and willows glow yellow, gold and orange, and soon the whole tundra is a tapestry of warm colors.

Sedges, small woody plants, and grasses are intertwined more commonly in other types of tundra, and in summer—when the alpine tundra is apt to provide a pleasant, springy carpet for a traveler to move across—the tussock country makes for slow and difficult going. Here big clumps of coarse grasses stand with their feet in water—and often the hiker does likewise. In wetter areas, the tundra gives way to bogs and muskegs when hot summer weather brings deeper thaws. The ground becomes soggy, its hummocks clothed with lush, feathery sphagnum mosses as well as the ubiquitous lichen and berries.

Much of Alaska—over 50 percent—is above tree line because of latitude, altitude, or climate. Thus, vast areas of western Alaska, although in the lower latitudes, are swept constantly by hard-driving winds and are as inhospitable to forests as the frigid North Slope or the high crags of the mountains. But inland, and south of the Arctic Divide, the trees begin to take hold. The tree of Alaska is the spruce.

In the harsher regions of the interior the black spruce is dominant, staking down the thin chill soils with its shallow root system, eking out a marginal existence in the often desperate cold. This tree has an unkempt look about it; it has short, shaggy branches that clothe its flagpole-straight trunk almost evenly so that it appears nearly cylindrical but for its pointed tip. So dark a green that it seems black—as its name indicates—this stiff, erect, and sturdy tree of the sparse boreal forest may punctuate a stretch of tundra, standing above a swath of bright berries and dwarf willows. It may grow in company with birch and poplar and, occasionally, the larch. But it thrives best in the marshes and muskegs, where it forms a distinctive community of its own, the black spruce bog. Threaded into the wet, mossy floors of these boggy forests may be the lovely, carnivorous sundew as well as the delicious bog cranberry.

The small size of the black spruce trees in open country is often deceptive; they may appear to be quite youthful, being short and heavily tufted with needles. But like the conifers of high elevations, these trees may be two centuries old or more, stunted by the rigorous climate.

In parts of the interior where the roots of trees can reach deeper, forests of white spruce and birch make a typical taiga community. The white spruce is more handsome than the black, its ashy brown buttressed boll gaining substanial girth through the decades, its trunk towering sixty to seventy feet or more above a moss and lichen covered forest floor. This spruce bears its beautiful, pendulous purple cones near the tip of its crown, and its limber branches spread into thickly needled fans, which catch and hold the snow. Each twig is armored with prickly dark blue-green needles which are, in fact, the leaves of the tree. The needles fade and fall in a continuous gentle drift to form a thick brown mat around the tree's patterned trunk. In autumn the birches flame with color and the white spruce interlaced among them seem to glow an even deeper blue-green.

Along Alaska's southern coastal areas, where the climate is more equable, the forests thicken. Sitka spruce thrives with the western hemlock in this warmer, wetter region. Together they form a wide band of lush forest growth that arcs along the shore of the Gulf of Alaska all the way to Afognak Island just off Kodiak. When left alone, these forests clothe all parts of the lowlands, including the countless islands of the Inside Passage as well as the sloping shores of the mainland. They grow in stands so dense that only a green-gold glow of light can penetrate to their deep, mossy floors. Occasionally tall, fragrant cedars drape their graceful branches through the shadows, and dogwood grows in thick clusters in the understory. The blueberries here can slow a late-summer traveler, and the deceptively handsome devil's club can stop one altogether with its wicked thorns.

These beautiful mixed forests flourish around the mouth of Glacier Bay, an area that was covered by glaciers only 200 years ago. A trip through the National Monument up the bay to the terminal moraines of the present glaciers offers an interesting exhibit of the natural succession of the plants that follow the retreat of a glacier in southeast Alaska. It is a trip backwards in botanical time. From the lush climax forests, established successfully after two centuries, the forest cover dwindles steadily up the course of the bay. The towering spruce and hemlock give way to stands of cottonwood, a hardier species, and then to thickets of alder. At the bay's head, in the loose unstable rubble of the glaciers' recently piled-up moraines, the delicate-looking dryas and the showier alpine epilobium lift up their blossoms, signaling the first toehold of life in the newly formed rocky soil. Each sturdy pioneer plant prepares the way for the one that follows. Unless the glaciers advance again, in 200 years a mixed spruce-hemlock forest may well tower where now the low-growing dryas and epilobium bend before the summer breezes.

Alaska's official state flower is the pale blue forget-me-not. But the flower seen most commonly in Alaska—and almost everywhere in this vigorous and changing country—is the fireweed, the epilobium. Found here in two varieties, the tall, plumy *Epilobium angustifolium* which grows in the lower altitudes, and the hardier alpine form, *Epilobium latifolium*, which is lower and bushier, this is the pioneer plant that moves in following any disturbance or wounding of the land. Whether the ground is charred by fire, scraped by a glacier, laid open by a bulldozer, or sloughed off in a landslide, the fireweed comes to clothe the bare soil. In some places it grows so thickly, particularly after a fire, that it paints the whole landscape a soft cerise.

Each of Alaska's plant communities supports a particular animal community, a number of creatures that have evolved to take advantage of the particular kind of food supply. Some of the animals are vegetarians, others carnivores, and some of the most successful are, like man, omnivores, taking both plants and other animals for their food. In much of Alaska the plant and animal communities still live together in undisturbed, dynamic interdependence. And since each is necessary to the other, the success of the total community varies with the success of its different members. For example, the population of the Brown and Collared lemmings that occupy the Arctic regions oscillates wildly, and so do the numbers of their mammalian and avian predators. (This particular instance of natural interrelationship—now so rarely witnessed—is in the words of one biologist, "one of the most exciting natural phenomena on earth.") In another example of interdependence, both bear and beluga whales use salmon for food and they suffer when populations of this anadromous fish decline. But here man is also a competitor: he controls the destiny of all three species.

Alaska's animals depend, of course, on the special environment as much as they do on the special kinds of food the land provides. Many of them have evolved with the requirement of vast space through which to range. Thus, in Alaska's wilderness areas are some of the last large populations of earth's great mammals, creatures that must have freedom and wide territory for survival. Many of these animals were once common throughout the lower North American continent, but crowded by man and his artifacts, brought down by his bullets for his food, poisoned because of their habits, trapped for their fur, their habitat destroyed, they are now all but gone. Become unfamiliar or even forgotten they exist there mostly as objects of curiosity in a local zoo. Doomed to eventual extinction in a world too "civilized" to include them, they are making their final stand in Alaska. Seen here in their natural environment they are awesome reminders of the extraordinary richness, diversity, and beauty of life. As wild and free and magnificent as the land itself, they embody the living spirit of this last great wilderness.

Among them are numerous ungulates or grazers, animals that support an often considerable bulk on small leafy plants. The incredibly swift and nimble mountain goats, and the Dall sheep, which may freeze momentarily into perfect white statues, roam the high reaches of most of Alaska's great mountains. The fleet-footed blacktail deer thrives on the rich browse of the southeast. The moose—a species that looks as impressive and improbable as the wooly mammoth and the sabre-toothed tiger and is just as old—find the lush willows and other plants of wet places in almost every part of the state. (Although comparatively sparse in earlier periods, the moose is presently one of Alaska's most successful mammals, comprising an estimated 85 to 95 percent of its biomass.)

The tundra is home for the caribou, which depend primarily on the leafy lichen for their food, although they are not averse to the tender green shoots of dwarf birch and poplar. They require large quantities of their tiny browse. The Arctic Herd, for example, which numbers near 300,000 animals, must range for hundreds of miles from the Arctic shore to south of the Arctic Circle. The animals move back and forth across great stretches of space, pulled first north and then south by the change of the seasons, trotting across the vast tundra plains and the rolling foothills and filing through the mountain passes to find their particular wintering grounds and calving grounds. To see them in full migratory flood is to witness a surge of life as elemental and irresistible as the surge of a great river; they stream by in seemingly infinite numbers, tens of thousands of animals, each moved by an urge as ancient as their species.

Among the most spectacular of Alaska's wild creatures are the bears—the black bear, which in parts of the southeast has a deep blue cast to its coat; the glacier bear which lives along the ice fields; the brown bear of the coastal regions and its cousin, the grizzly of the interior; and the creamy white polar bear of the Arctic. The larger species of these great animals, the brown bear and the polar, weigh more than three-fourths of a ton and are so huge that they stand five feet tall when on all fours and rise ten feet when they rear up. To confront such an animal straight on is an unforgettable experience which can leave a human feeling small indeed—one reason why men have so consistently hunted out the bears and tried to kill them. For these bears, like many humans, will not attack unless they are threatened or crowded, or their territory is invaded (accidentally or otherwise, it should be noted). It seems incongruous that so large a beast can make do on a diet of roots and berries and small rodents, but many do. Those along the coast, of course, are expert fishermen. Like people, they crowd the banks of streams when the salmon run. In the Arctic, the polar bears make their way across the ice, lumbering nimbly despite their bulk—to find an open spot of water for their fishing.

In the thaw lakes and ponds of Alaska it is not uncommon to see the sleek dark head of a muskrat cutting a V-shaped wake into the glassy waters as it swims by. Or the watcher may find the bright, alert eyes of a beaver, safe in the shelter of a well-built lodge, returning his gaze. The little ground squirrels are bold and unafraid, and the red squirrels of the taiga fill the air with the clatter of their voices. These forest sentinels inhabit a three-dimensional world, leaping from crown to crown of the white spruce, scurrying up and down the tree trunks, building their middens on the forest floor, and snoozing away the winter under a blanket of snow.

They are bound to the land, all these wild animals—and the many others that inhabit Alaska—being dependent upon certain foods and a particular kind of habitat. But they are also part of the larger fabric of life which extends into Alaska's waters, into her skies, and eventually into the whole biosphere. For example, the land animals concentrate the nutrients essential for life in their bodies and upon their death the decomposers unravel these nutrients and return them to the ground and its waters; eventually many of those nutrients will be washed into the sea to provide nourishment for marine life. In turn, the anadromous fish—in the ecologists' classic demonstration of the interrelatedness of all living things—carry the nutrients of the ocean inland to the place of their birth in their own bodies; again the nutrients are released and taken up by other forms of life, perhaps in a leafing willow which will feed a moose, and eventually, a man. There are other, more subtle links between the various forms of life which we are only dimly beginning to comprehend. In every level of its environment, Alaska offers one of earth's last relatively undisturbed laboratories where the elemental secrets of life may still be explored.

The Alaskan coastal waters are of special interest to many biologists and ecologists, for they are extraordinarily productive. Conservationist John P. Milton considers Bristol Bay and the Gulf of Alaska "among the finest marine biological zones in the world." In part, the cold water which traps certain important nutrients is responsible. But in addition, there is the wealth of nutrients carried into Alaska's great estuarine and coastal areas by some of the continent's major rivers. The offshore waters can literally teem with life.

The marine food chain, like the terrestrial, starts with the green plants which take the sun's energy and use it to manufacture food. The phytoplankton—or microscopic floating plants—thrive in the arctic waters, enriching them with enormous "crops" of food. Along with the seaweeds, they are the basis for an extensive and varied marine food chain. Many fish and shellfish graze directly on the plants and the organic material which they provide, from the tiny shrimp or krill which feed in turn the baleen whale to the crabs which grow to such remarkable size and succulence that they are sent all over the world for gourmet tables. Other members of the marine community are the anadromous fish, which have historically occurred in remarkable variety and number. These are the arctic char, the grayling, a whole spectrum of trout, and of course, the salmon. The quantity of salmon in Alaska streams was awesome less than a century ago. In 1880 John Muir visited a stream in the southeast and recorded the following scene:

"As for the salmon, as seen this morning urging their way up the swift current—tens of thousands of them, side by side, with their backs out of the water in shallow places now that the tide was low—nothing that I could write might possibly give anything like a fair conception of the extravagance of their numbers. There was more salmon, apparently, bulk for bulk, than water in the stream. The struggling multitudes, crowding one against the other, could not get out of our way when we waded into the midst of them. . . . " Similar scenes could have been described at the mouth of almost every river emptying into the Alaskan coast that year.

After decades of uncontrolled commercial exploitation, the salmon runs are now greatly diminished, and certain species—such as the reds—have been all but fished out. Nonetheless, it is still possible to witness the extraordinary bounty of nature when the salmon find their way inland each year. Crowds of them darken the mouth of every stream that feeds the lyrically beautiful clear lakes of the Wood River-Tikchik country in western Alaska. Swarms of bright red fish push their way through the estuaries and bays and leap valiantly up the falls of Kenai's Russian River, Katmai's Brooks River, the fish ladders of the mighty Yukon— virtually every coastal waterway.

Even as Alaska's land is home now for some of the last large populations of terrestrial mammals, her shores are home for some of the last great congregations of earth's marine mammals. Along the Alaskan coasts there are still crowds of the Pacific walrus, the north fur seal, the ringed seal, the "ugruk," the huge bearded seal that can weigh as much as 800 pounds, and the beluga, the white whale which chases the salmon inland. Huge herds of sea lions cavort on the coastal rocks. Pods of great whales arc majestically through Alaska's blue bays as they travel southward, their black bodies frosted with barnacles, gleaming in the slanting sunlight. Tawny walrus pack themselves tightly onto the islands off Bristol Bay, crowding every inch of available space; one moves and the others follow in an irresistible flow of life as they gain the water, leaving only empty rocks behind. If a watcher is fortunate, there is a chance to witness the playful fur seals in their unique ballets, or a sea otter lolling on his back, a mollusk in his flippers, floating contentedly with the changing tide. The sight of any of these animals can have the same strong sensory impact on the observer as the sight of migrating caribou.

The cliffs and shores of Alaska also provide the rookeries for literally millions of seabirds; for murres and puffins, auklets and guillemots, gulls, kittiwakes, and cormorants—all avian creatures of fascinating habit and design. Possibly the most overwhelming and moving display of wildlife in Alaska, in fact, occurs in the prodigious number of birds that surge in migratory tides to the Alaskan coasts and inland areas every year, marking the elemental revolution of the seasons. Each spring and fall, wave after wave of avian travelers crowd the skies, the sound of wild songs and thousands of wingbeats filling the air. Knowing in ways we do not comprehend which celestial pathway to take, the different species move unerringly to their chosen place—on a particular coastal cliff, in a rich delta or inland wetland, along the shore of a particular lake or stream, or in a special part of the tundra. There, as does all other life in Alaska, the migratory birds live intensely, purposefully, and gloriously through the few bright summer months.

Thus, the small shorebirds that nest on the Arctic tundra, lining their nests with wisps of dry willow catkins and downy dryas, may brood their eggs for twenty-four days. But two hours after the young have pipped, the tiny "instant birds" can tumble from the nest and wobble around. Less than a day later, they are running across the ground. Another three weeks and the babies are able to fly, preparing for the long trek southward as the nights grow longer.

Along with the birds of the tundra and other inland areas, and adding to the millions of seabirds that populate the Alaskan coasts, at least 13 million waterfowl feed and nest in Alaska's wetlands and river deltas. Their greatest concentrations occur on the Arctic Slope and coast—where all of Canada's eider ducks and many other waterfowl species nest—and in the wetlands of the Yukon Flats and the Yukon-Kuskokwim delta.

The Yukon Flats stretch over almost 11,000 square miles, an area of seemingly infinite lakes and ponds and scrolling streams interlocked with islands, spurs, and peninsulas of dark spruce forest. Along with notably frigid winters, this interior region has hot summers, and many lightning-caused fires which increase the fertility of the soil. The plant life on the land and in the water is exceptionally rich and varied, and so is the animal life. Fish flash among the yellow pond lilies which float on the still, tea-colored waters; bears amble through the tall grasses and feast among the thick tangle of blueberries. Moose clamber over the sphagnum moss to gain the cover of the heavy forests. The wild cry of a loon may follow the call of a wolf. In this setting, many species of duck—widgeon, teal, canvasback, mallard, pintail, and scaup among them—join with the loons, geese, and grebes to nest by the hundreds of thousands.

The Yukon-Kuskokwim delta is Alaska's largest wetland, alone supporting at least 2 million waterfowl. Countless tarns, lakes, streams, and curls of old meanders dot and streak this delta's treeless landscape. The edges of the wetter places are outlined with plants of darker green than the soft gray-green of the continuously interrupted marshland and tundra. A pair of whistler swans may nestle against the edge of any little pond, or a gaggle of geese feed contentedly along the shore, their softly brown-striped bodies blending with the muddy sand. This is the nesting place of almost all of North America's emperor geese and cackling geese, as well as half of the continent's black brant. Many other species of geese, ducks, swans, loons, and cranes crowd the clear, pale spring and autumn skies as they move on their great migratory journeys.

The flyways of these birds, and all the others that summer in Alaska, fan out in all directions. The shorebird born on the Arctic tundra may fly south as far as Patagonia before winter comes. The lesser yellowlegs, which screams imprecations at an intruder to its summer sanctuary on Takahula Lake in the Brooks Range, may head for another place in South America. The mew gull with a nest within sight of Mt. McKinley may winter in San Francisco, while jaegers that swoop along the coast of the Arctic Ocean will travel instead to Japan. The wheatear seen in the rolling hills near Nome prefers to winter in tropical Africa. The arctic tern, which reared its young along the shores of the Delta River, may migrate to the Antarctic. Birds from every continent depend upon Alaska for their survival: it is a heartland for the avian populations of the planet.

While wild Alaska may be a paradise for many kinds of animals, it is not an easy place—especially in the Arctic regions—for humans to live. It takes a particular quality of spirit to endure the unrelenting cold of the northern winters, the pure and powerful presence of the persistent snowy darkness, where the blue-black starry arch of sky is stabbed by the northern lights. It requires physical strength as well, a healthy body, powerful will, and stamina simply to get around the place, let alone wrest a living from it. And it takes ingenuity to adapt to the living conditions and to utilize an often unstable food supply.

Yet people have been living in Alaska for thousands of years. Sealed away in flows of lava and volcanic ash are tools and other relics of cultures that date back at least 10,000 years. Some anthropologists believe man first arrived here perhaps 40,000 years ago. Much of the evidence, including lichen-covered cairns on the tops of coastal hills and craters, is clustered along the western shores of Alaska. It is believed people reached this area via the land bridge that linked the North American continent to Eurasia in periods of heavy glaciation when the sea was lowered. It is likely that bands of nomads followed the woolly mammoths, antelope, bison, mastodon, camel, and sabertooth tiger—the unbelievable large fauna which thrived in Alaska until about 6000 B.C.

Many of those early peoples moved on, but some remained. Among them were four groups with different languages and customs who made their peace with the land they found. The Eskimos, a coastal people and skilled hunters, stayed largely in the north and northwest, principally along the shore, setting up winter and summer camps as they followed their game, gathering berries in the waning summer days. Adaptable, pragmatic people, they built their houses from the sod, used birds and fish for their subsistence as well as mammals of both the land and the sea—the caribou, fox, bear, walrus, seal, and whale. They were carvers of exceptional artistry, especially of animals, and used both bone and ivory for their work. They helped pass the long, dark winter months with dances which embodied their history as well as their customs and beliefs.

A second group, the Athapaskans, went inland. Some crossed the continent and settled around what would later be known as Hudson Bay. Others filtered into the central United

States to become the progenitors of the Apaches and Navajos. Still others stayed in the subarctic interior to live a nomadic existence, in part along the banks of the rivers they traveled, the Yukon and Porcupine among them. With ritual apologies, they killed the bear and moose and caribou for their food and clothing. They were skilled trackers of game, using snowshoes in the winter months, and building snug trail shelters of snow as well as devising tents from animal skins. Along with the Eskimos they smoked their salmon to preserve them and made good use of the climate's—and the permafrost's—deep-freeze qualities for preserving their berries and game. And like the Eskimos, they lived in a close-knit cooperative society, sharing their food, clothing, and even their few personal belongings, and rearing their children as important and responsible members of the family and the group.

Another people, the Aleuts, with a language and customs fundamentally similar to those of the Eskimos, turned southward and westward on their trek, occupying the Alaskan peninsula and the Aleutian Island chain. They made their homes along the shores and lakes and gave a name to the place they lived, Alaska, the Great Land. Although their "iglus" and villages were repeatedly sifted over with volcanic ash, they relocated nearby, taking advantage of the enormously productive coastal waters.

Moving further to the east and south along the shores, the Tlingits, Haidas, and similar Indian tribes came to flourish along the heavily forested shores, forming the northern section of what was possibly the second largest aboriginal settlement on the North American continent. (Related peoples occupied the coastal areas south into what is now California.) In an easier climate and with a bountiful food supply, they gathered material wealth, developed distinctive art forms and sophisticated legal and social structures, which included the unique practice of the "potlatch," a ceremony whereby wealthier members of the tribe obligated others through the giving of gifts.

All of these native peoples depended for food, in one degree or another, upon the salmon, which swarmed along their shores and up their rivers. All were skilled hunters of the large land and sea mammals, which gave them both food and clothing. And all of them developed rich cultural heritages of drum-dancing and oral literatures.

Although there is some evidence that the demise of much of the highly varied earlier fauna was man-caused, most of the Alaskan peoples, in historic times at least, seem to have existed in relative balance with their environment. Until the coming of the white man they were hunters and fishermen who rarely took more than they needed and wasted no part of what they took. Although they traded among themselves, it was usually more for the purpose of sharing amenities and necessities than for gaining material wealth. Their greatest treasures were immaterial—such things as special rights and privileges, and even songs. And while they differed in many of their ways, and sometimes warred with one another, they shared some basic concepts. Among these was a respect for the land and the life it supported. The land was not the private property of an individual; rather, the land, its waters, and occasionally parts of the ocean, were recognized as the hunting territory of a family or a group. The concept of exploiting the land was alien. The use of the land was a precious heirloom, to be cherished and passed on to following generations.

The white men, however, brought a different culture to Alaska, a very different set of "philosophies, desires, and yearnings," as scientist Richard Cooley puts it. They came at first as explorers, for the glory of their homelands, and always seeking treasure. They believed that any land they found was theirs to take and exploit and so was anything on it or in it. Implicit in their philosophy was the idea that if they used up a resource—whether fur seal, gold, or salmon—they would simply move on and find another.

They came early from Europe, from Spain, and England, but the first to colonize the land were the Russians. Arriving in the mid-eighteenth century from the west, they moved along the shores, and from the Seward Peninsula south they built their forts and then their churches. By the nineteenth century they had, nominally at least, subdued the Tlingit and Haida Indians in the south and despite a background of bitter hatreds and bloodshed, they were making

Sitka—or "New Archangel"—into a miniature "Paris of the Pacific." Before many decades had passed the Russian colonists had nearly exterminated the fur seal, the sea otter, and the Aleuts, whom they enslaved and infected with their diseases.

A century after their arrival, with their lucrative fur resources almost gone, it was clear to the Russians that they had overextended themselves in Alaska. Their colonies were too far from home, and Alaska was not a place to be easily tamed. By the time Secretary of State William H. Seward was ready to buy Alaska for the United States, Russia was ready to sell. In consummating the deal—for the sum of $7.2 million—it seemed unimportant that the Native peoples did not formally relinquish their rights to the land that was their aboriginal home. Congress could always take care of the matter at a later date.

The purchase of Alaska in 1867 was the United States' last large land acquisition, the final surge of the tide of western expansion. (It was hoped that, along with providing mineral and forest resources, the new territory would also provide ground for laying the lines of the new international cable being pushed by the American Telegraph Company.) It was not a particularly popular acquisition. The United States was trying to heal the wounds of a devastating civil war, and the country west of the Mississippi was challenge enough for the times. Besides, Alaska was largely unexplored by white men, unmapped, and generally unknown. It was widely believed to be a vast, snowbound wasteland, worthless and barren of life except for a few polar bears, walrus, and aborigines living in igloos. "Seward's Icebox" was a common name for the new territory, or "Icebergia," "Walrussia," or more unkindly "Seward's Folly." (Seward, however, knew better. He considered the acquisition of Alaska the crowning achievement of his career. He also recognized that it would take a long time for people to accept the fact.) The first census of Alaska, in 1880, thirteen years after its purchase showed a total of 33,426 persons of whom only 430 were not indigenous.

In this critical period of American history the giveaway of public lands was seen as a logical means of developing new country. Seaward, however, at first excluded Alaska from the land laws that applied to the contiguous states. Not until 1884, when Alaska was made a District and the Mining Laws of 1874 were amended, was the territory opened to prospecting. And not until 1890 was it possible to homestead Alaskan land. Generally tailored to fit the terrain of the eastern United States, the requirements of the Homestead Act proved to be ludicrously unsuited to Alaskan conditions. Few homesteaders then or later were able to prove up their land without federal assistance. The Trade and Manufacturing Sites Act of 1891, passed with the salmon-cannery industry in mind, offered 80 acres of public land for a minimum purchase price to anyone setting up a business, but most businessmen of that time were occupied elsewhere

Many accounts of Alaska—often glowing—were brought back by a series of hardy explorers, some privately financed, but most working under the aegis of the federal government. One of the most extraordinary exploratory outings of that or any other time occurred just before the turn of the century, when railroad magnate Edward Harriman funded an expedition which was ostensibly a family holiday and hunting party. With it went scores of luminaries and scientists, chosen in cooperation with the Smithsonian Institute and the Washington Academy of Sciences. Their resulting twelve-volume report, the *Harriman Alaska Expedition*, still remains a mine of valuable information. There was also a small and steady stream of adventurous tourists who took the steamer through Alaska's southeast. Still, there was no stampede to the new territory until 1898. Then the discovery of gold brought the first major influx of "cheechakos." Tough, fearless, and often avaricious, miners swarmed inland and down the Yukon and its tributaries, performing prodigious feats in their search for treasure. They dragged their iron stoves across the icecaps, nailed together shaky craft and traveled the wild rivers in hair-raising voyages, and grappled with grizzlies and sometimes won and sometimes lost. They left a colorful and violent history, and to the natives an even richer legacy of another white man's disease—already present in Alaska—alchoholism.

It is estimated that about 200,000 ambitious souls started for the gold fields of the Yukon, and later Nome, but only 50,000 stuck to the arduous quest. When the gold was gone, many of them moved on, but some stayed. And by 1910, the population, at 63,356, had almost doubled, and the non-Natives outnumbered the Natives by nearly 8 to 5.

Still, only a few mining and homestead claims were scattered across Alaska when the federal government in 1912 established Alaska officially as a Territory. In the meantime Washington had initiated the subdivision of Alaskan land. First to be set aside from public entry were nearly 21 million acres of forested land in southeast and south central Alaska; some 16 million acres went into the Tongass Forest, the rest into the Chugach. Subsequent federal withdrawals went on as the century progressed; Katmai National Monument, Mt. McKinley National Park, Glacier Bay National Monument—in all some 7 million acres of land of "most unusual natural beauty" went into the National Park system. (The choice of these areas can be considered arbitrary, too. In the words of an Anchorage resident, "the whole state meets the criteria of National Park designation.") More or less extensive tracts successively came under administration of the Bureau of Sport Fisheries and Wildlife which today administers 19 million acres. Substantial areas were set aside for power purposes, and more loosely for the use of the Natives, although Congress continued to let the years go by without settling the question of the Natives' land rights.

While some federal reservations involved chunks of land as large as or larger than many of the lower contiguous states, they attracted little general attention to the Territory. The establishment of the National Parks may have added to the tourism, but most of Alaska remained unknown for decades. It was a long way off, hard to get to and harder to get around in, even when the days of the bush pilot came to be. Until World War II, the Territory went its lonely, remote, essentially unspoiled way, its population increasing so gradually that it had reached only 75,524 in 1942, the Natives totalling about 33,000—essentially the same number as in 1880.

It is noteworthy that throughout these earlier decades, the Alaskan Natives escaped some of the more traditional traumas of colonization. Under United States administration there was not the bloodletting that occurred under the Russian; the American military charged with various administrative chores had in fact come into little actual conflict with the Natives. While Congress had not defined their land rights, the Alaskans were not dispossessed and herded into alien reservations, as were so many indigenous peoples in other parts of the continent. For the most part they continued to occupy their ancestral territories and to speak their Native tongues. A number of their traditions prevailed; subsistence hunting and fishing, for instance, remained integral and necessary parts of their way of life. And, like any white Alaskan, the Native was accorded the full rights of citizenship, including voting privileges.

The Alaskan Natives were not immune, however, to other, sometimes subtler effects of a colonial society. It would take many decades for them to accommodate to the white man's diseases; well into the twentieth century a small village could be wiped out by an epidemic of measles or influenza. Too, many well-meaning members of the Bureau of Indian Affairs—and of many churches—often considered the Native people uncivilized, uneducated, and unsaved. Many cheechakos did their best to civilize, educate, and save them, each according to his own particular ideas and standards. (The Federal Council of Churches early allotted various regions of Alaska to different sects for their missionary work; thus the area of the Brooks Range, Anaktuvak Pass, Barrow, and Wainwright went first to the Presbyterians; the Point Hope and Point Lay regions went to the Episcopalians, and so forth.) Soon the summer camps and hunting villages gave way to more highly organized communities with a post office and a school, where the classes were often taught in English, complete with "Dick and Jane" books. Dancing was frowned upon by many of the missionaries (who were often medical) and so the community lodges, sites of much Native life, were abandoned. Now the people gathered together in the new churches, or in the National Guard armories.

There occurred inevitably an erosion of the Native cultures. And despite their training in the white man's language and his ways, the Alaskan people were not fully accepted into the white man's society. Forced into an economic system alien to most of them (the Tlingits, Haidas, and other southeastern Indians could more readily identify with it), they found there were not many jobs for them. There were not many jobs for anyone in Alaska, as a matter of fact. Short of trapping, fishing, or prospecting—all seasonal and all uncertain—work for pay was hard to come by. Mining was always a white hope, but generally turned out to be a way of life rather than a profit-making venture. Most people with regular salaries were employed by the government, and the federal government did try to pump funds into the Alaskan economy.

Many of the federal projects were of the usual and expected order; the government built what roads there were, constructed and operated a railroad, and in places erected hospitals as well as schools. Some of its projects, however, were more imaginative; the government tried early to set up the Arctic Eskimos in business—the business of raising reindeer for profit. Using the same browse as the caribou, the reindeer displaced the indigenous animals. Their population peaked and then crashed; only a few herds remained and the Eskimos did not take easily to being herdsmen.

In the mid-thirties, along with initiating a number of welfare programs, the government also tried to bring commercial farming to Alaska. In an immensely costly experiment, dust-bowl farmers were transplanted from the Midwest to the Matanuska Valley. Only a handful of hardy souls survived. And while they learned to grow cabbages four feet in diameter, most of their vegetables were inferior, and far more expensive, than those that were brought in from the "lower 48." (According to recent estimates, there are still well under 100 square miles in all of Alaska where commercial agriculture enjoys any degree of success.)

While no bombs fell on the Alaska mainland during World War II, the war had an incalculable effect, causing profound changes. Because of Alaska's strategic location (the Aleutian chain stops just 1,000 miles short of Japan, the Seward Peninsula just 56 miles from Russia), the military practically seized it. They poured billions of dollars—and billions of yards of concrete—into it. Roads (including the beginnings of the Alcan highway), airfields, weather stations, military bases, housing, office buildings and other military structures were constructed where wilderness had been before.

Along with causing a major building boom, World War II brought about much more comprehensive and detailed mapping of the terrain and more thorough geological exploration. The latter resulted in the withdrawal of another 24 million acres of federal land, the establishment of the Navy's Petroleum No. 4 oil reserve on the Arctic Slope. (Military activities also resulted in the littering of countless 55 gallon oil drums over millions of acres of Arctic landscape, along with an enduring network of "cat" tracks on the tundra.)

Alaska's population and economy soared. In the two decades following 1940, the number of residents tripled, with military personnel and their dependents accounting for over one fourth of the total. When Alaska achieved statehood in 1958—after years of local effort—the population stood at nearly 230,000. By then, however, the military boom was going bust; the new state had a perilously narrow economic base. After almost a century of heavy, steady fishing, its prodigious salmon resource was on the wane, and the southeast was turning to the cutting of its forests under the aegis of the United States Forest Service. (It did not cause much concern locally, or nationally, that most of the logs—and the dollars—went out of the country.) Gas and oil explorations in the Cook Inlet were beginning to pay off. Oil had been detected on the North Slope in seeps as early as 1903, and the Navy's "Pet 4" withdrawal was further testimony to its presence there, but only explorations were going on in the Arctic regions. There was still hope for other mineral discoveries, but they had not yet materialized. There were pressures for power development. (These peaked in 1965, when 23 million acres of land went into the incredible Rampart withdrawal, a project that would have flooded an area the size of Lake Erie and incidentally drowned the Yukon Flats, destroying one of the world's important wildlife resources.) Tourism was becoming an increasingly lucrative business. Yet with all the possibilities, the reduction of the military infusion left the unemployment rate high and rising, and Alaska faced what some called a financial crisis.

Aware of Alaska's chronic economic problems, as well as its great potential, Congress wrote the Alaska Statehood Law with a lavish hand and set into motion a second major subdivision of the Alaskan land. In 1958 about 74 percent of Alaska, some 262,800,000 acres, was considered "vacant, unappropriated, and unreserved" public domain. (Only 0.2 percent of the Territory was in private hands, the almost 26 percent that remained—about 92 million acres—had been withdrawn by the federal government.) From this, the state of Alaska was given the right to "select" for its own some 103,600,000 acres, an area greater in size than the entire state of California. Another 400,000 state acres were to come from U.S. Forest Service lands. Full title to the fabulous Alaska tidelands—another 35,000,000 to 45,000,000 acres—swelled the total of the new state's lands to nearly 150 million acres.

This enormous land grant, larger than the combined federal land grants to all seventeen western states, was an unprecedented dowry. Tying off the package were two big bows: the title to all minerals in state-selected lands would remain with the state; thus, Alaska leases, but does not sell, the rights to the oil, gas, phosphate, coal, and other resources found in state lands. And, in contrast to all other states, Alaska receives 90 percent of the *federal* revenues from mineral leasing on public-domain lands within its boundaries. As Cooley writes with considerable understatement: "Congress has indeed been generous with Alaska."

Not the least of the benefits given Alaska in the enactment of its statehood was the rare chance to pioneer in new approaches to land use and development, to build into the exploitation of the land some measure of protection and understanding. By the terms of statehood, the means were there. But most Alaskans, including many key decision-makers, were too deeply steeped in the earlier pioneer tradition of taking all they could get and hopefully striking it rich. And while the new state struggled to establish itself, Washington had to remain the single largest economic contributor. Even in 1965, it poured one half billion dollars into the state. This money, like all the rest that has so long flowed into Alaska, came from the pockets of the American taxpayer, who has historically seemed unaware of his considerable financial stake in this state.

The establishment of Alaskan statehood, like the acquisition of Alaska itself, occurred at a critical time in United States history. In the early '60s powerful changes were beginning to leaven American society. Among others, civil rights and poverty were emerging as major political issues. In this climate, the Alaska Statehood Law proved to be less than the panacea some had hoped it would be. For in writing the legislation, the Congress had once again sidestepped the issue of Native land claims and failed to define the aboriginal rights to the "vacant and unappropriated" public domain from which the state would select its land. Now when the Natives, a minority group with many of its members living in what white society would characterize as abject poverty, began to assert their rights, people—importantly, politicians—began to listen and respond.

And by the early sixties, after a century of indoctrination, the Alaskan Natives were proving that some of them had learned the white man's ways unexpectedly well. Their value system had undergone change; so had their "desires, philosophies, and yearnings." Now not only did they want their aboriginal lands—they wanted money as well. One of the first native challenges to state selections occurred on the Arctic Slope where the presence of petroleum was being confirmed; the selection involved traditional hunting territory, and the Natives' lawyer argued that the natives—not the state—should get the money for exploration rights. Not having relinquished their aboriginal title, they turned out to be on firm legal ground. This particular protest involved some 96 million acres of land.

Finding themselves with increasing and unusual political clout, the Natives continued to press their claims. The federal government was able to negotiate and settle with the Tlingits and Haidas. But the demands of the Eskimos, Aleuts, and Athapaskans, who set aside their traditional internal differences to form the Alaskan Federation of Natives in 1966, were considered too high. The AFN first claimed title to 125 million acres as their "public domain." (By 1967, the figure had risen to the total acreage of Alaska.) In December 1966, Secretary of the Interior Stewart Udall reacted by instituting a "freeze" on the disposition of all Alaskan lands, halting homesteading along with federal withdrawals and state selections, pending Congressional settlement of the now formal Native Claims.

Meantime conservationists—themselves in a position of growing political power—were becoming aware of Alaska and beginning to explore this last great wilderness of the United States. What they saw both excited and appalled them; here was clearly the country's greatest scenic and wildlife resource, and the land and its resources were in all too many places being exploited with the same carelessness, profligacy, and resultant destruction accorded the West a hundred years ago. National conservation leaders launched a major campaign to protect and preserve Alaska's invaluable resources.

Into this complex situation, already loaded with potential as well as active conflicts, the news of a major oil strike at Prudhoe Bay flared like a rocket in the summer of 1968. It set off a variety of reactions, from wild elation to profound apprehension. The state saw Prudhoe Bay as the answer to its economic woes. Many Alaskans saw it as the long-awaited chance to get rich themselves. The oil interests saw it as a bonanza. Some of the Natives viewed it as a further challenge to their rights. And conservationists saw it as a major threat of destruction to both the great land and the life it supported.

In the ensuing scramble to get the oil out immediately—the necessity of which was an *a priori* assumption on the part of most people concerned—the oil companies holding leases on the North Slope (led by Atlantic Richfield, British Petroleum, and Humble) formed a consortium to build an 800-mile pipeline from Prudhoe Bay to Valdez, which was considered the most usable and accessible ice-free port although it was the epicenter of the 1964 earthquake. Ignoring the implications of the still-active land freeze and the fact that federal permission to build such a pipeline had not been granted, the consortium promptly ordered millions of dollars—and 800 miles—worth of forty-eight-inch diameter pipe in sections forty feet long. Japanese interests were the only ones willing and able to meet the specifications. The consortium then proceeded to lay out the route of the pipeline or TAPS, the Trans Alaskan Pipeline System, and to set up eight construction camps, like small trailer cities, in what had been some of Alaska's most superlative wilderness. The state cooperated enthusiastically. It sold Arctic land to the oil companies for $5 an acre for an anticipated city at Prudhoe Bay. (This land turned out to be unexpectedly rich in oil.) Retaining the permanent mineral rights, the state leased these rights for $900 million, only the beginning of revenues expected from future developments. Then-governor Walter E. Hickel pushed through the "Hickel Highway" the so-called "winter road" which bisected the Brooks Range at Anaktuvak Pass. Trucks lined up and waited for weeks for its opening in March 1969. (Many of the vehicles were flown back to Fairbanks in cargo planes.) The summer thaw revealed the twin tracks, or canals, they had carved through the muskeg and tundra.

Job hunters poured into the state, and the 1970 census revealed that there were 302,173 Alaskans, of whom just 50,819 were Native. (It is noteworthy, however, that in 1970 there were still only five towns with populations greater than 5,000.)

The Natives watched and waited. That year, when a group of conservationists sued to halt the construction of TAPS, a Native village joined them. To the surprise and consternation of many people, the federal courts held up the building of the pipeline because of the technicalities in an old law. Oil operations came to an abrupt halt. Although the pipe continued to pile up inexorably in Valdez, Fairbanks, and Prudhoe Bay, the construction camps along the pipeline route were quietly abandoned and the activity at Prudhoe Bay grew still. The scene of action shifted to Washington, D.C.

The legal aspects of building the pipeline would have to be resolved in Congress, and it would take three years, as it turned out. But in the meantime, it was essential to the oil consortium and to the state of Alaska that the "freeze" of Alaskan lands, extended under the Nixon administration, be thawed and the pattern of land ownership at last defined. Otherwise there would be a continuing threat of law suits and protests. The Native Claims, ignored by

Congress for over a century, would have to be settled, and politically, the timing seemed propitious.

With civil rights then a full-blown political issue, an Alaskan Native Claims settlement appeared to a number of concerned people to offer a way to right some of the white man's immemorial wrongs. And in the minds of a great many people, congressmen and senators included, most of Alaska was still a vast "empty" wilderness that could be dispensed with. On one score or another, it was possible to accept the argument that the Natives should have 40 million acres of land (and almost $1 billion as well) as fair recompense for their aboriginal rights. Greasing the legislative machinery with oil helped, too, to push through an act desired by a number of people for a number of different reasons. In October 1971 an unusual coalition of liberals working on behalf of the Natives, and conservatives working on behalf of the oil industry enacted the Alaskan Native Claims Settlement Act (known as ANCSA). After more than a century of foot-dragging, Congress passed this piece of legislation with remarkable dispatch. Conservationists who had long pushed for an equitable settlement for the Alaskan Natives had worked for broad land-use planning as an essential part of the Act, but land-use planning takes time, and the oil companies could not wait. The bill that went through so rapidly was inevitably both complex and confusing. It allowed only seven years for its terms to be met, and they would be seven lively years of argument and negotiations. By its terms, potentially the most devastating yet to the Alaskan land, the final disposition of this great territory would be achieved. And the lives of the Alaskan Natives would be profoundly and irrevocably changed.

In framing ANCSA, the Congress largely ignored the traditions and customs of the Native peoples—the land ethics on which they had based an earlier and remarkably successful existence, the historic philosophies and concepts that had guided and sustained them, even the long-established patterns of their subsistence hunting. The terms of the Act were a modern businessman's terms: ANCSA divided Alaska into twelve Regional Corporations, established to conduct "business for a profit." Each corporation has a Board of Directors, has issued common stock to all of its members, and is developing a program of investment for its corporate funds.

Inside the geographical area of each corporation there are a number of separate Village Corporations, one for each village. (A "village" consists of as few as twenty-five Natives living in the same place; a "Native" is a person who has at least one aboriginal grandparent.) Each village is entitled to "select" between three and seven townships (that is, between 69,120 and 161,280 acres), depending upon its population, out of the twenty-five townships immediately surrounding it. Ideally, each village's townships will be joined together to form a compact block, but in several instances this is not possible because of geography or previously patented land. To take care of such cases, ANCSA provides that the townships need not be contiguous but can touch corners only; or if this is not possible, a village can make up its "deficiencies" by selecting land lying some distance away. After the Village Corporations have patented their selections, the Regional Corporations will divide among them what is left of the 40 million acres of this Alaskan land grant. (About half of the nearly $1 billion bonus the Natives will receive will come from the general fund, i.e. from the United States taxpayers; the other half will come from Alaska's oil royalties.)

While the lands selected by the Natives and patented by them can remain in a kind of tax-free fund until 1991, at that time the corporations will dissolve; their shares and assets, including the land, will be issued to the stockholders who may dispose of them as they choose. Meantime, any patented lands may be sold by the corporations. And since the Regional Corporations are expected to show reasonable profits, economic development of one kind or another must proceed apace. Thus, the possible exploitation of mineral and forest resources has necessarily taken its place in the minds of many Natives, alongside the problems involved with traditional hunting. The conflicts of a people already in the grips of cultural change have inevitably been intensified.

Under the circumstances, it is not surprising that some of the Natives have responded by seeking to change the old ways as quickly and completely as possible. For example, if they have the money they may build a house that looks like an attractive California suburban home. Although its window walls may be heavy thermal glass, such a house will require a large output of energy to keep it warm, especially during Alaska's long frigid winters. Its neat modern kitchen and dinette will have no room for skinning a caribou or seal. Its flush toilet, perhaps one of the few around, will have the same problems of all flush toilets in the Arctic and sub-Arctic. The cost of building and maintaining such a house is high, by some Native standards, astronomical. But more significantly, its lines of support are stretched dangerously thin in a harsh environment. Without fuel, electricity, water, and garbage disposal, such a structure will be unlivable. And how to provide such amenities can be a planner's nightmare (and already is in many of Alaska's communities).

With the speeding up of the acculturation of the Native Alaskans, it is easy to find many who dress, speak, and seem to think, much like their white brothers. Most of them live in the state's few metropolitan areas; a number of them, too, have become the chosen leaders of their Corporations. Needing business managers, financial advisors, scientists, and lawyers more experienced than themselves, they have employed the sharpest experts they could find. And being human, they are taking every possible advantage of the financial opportunities offered in the frequently ambiguous phrasing of ANCSA. Some have arranged for leases with oil companies even before their land selections are designated, let alone patented. And while they cannot select lands aready conveyed to the state or those in existing National Parks, the Village Corporations have first choice of what is left, including limited selections inside the National Forests as well as the Wildlife Refuges. Many of their leaders, and non-Native advisors, mean to see them make the most of it.

Among other Natives, however, the attitudes are different; the changes will occur more slowly (but just as inevitably). There are still many Alaskan people, especially those in the outlying villages, who speak little or no English, who cling to their earlier customs, respecting the land and its resources. As they have for centuries, these people depend in large part upon subsistence hunting—of caribou, seals, moose, and birds—and berries for their food, although they may add fried chicken and canned corn to the evening meal. But the Native populations are growing, and so are the pressures on Alaska's wildlife. The Native Claims Act will increase the pressures as more and more land is subdivided and developed for profit. It is hard to predict how long subsistence hunting can remain a reality. It is hard, too, to predict how long stockholders in both Village and Regional Corporations can maintain a traditionally simple and uncluttered, albeit often rigorous way of life.

Many of their white friends want only the best for the Natives. "It would be great if every Native could have adequate health care, education, and housing—including modern plumbing," as one Alaskan put it. And then he added ruefully, "without the pressures, the stress, the complexities—the conflicts and problems which our sophisticated culture inevitably brings with it." It would also be nice, he might have noted, if the non-Natives could have the same lack of pretense, appreciation of the land and its resources, and capacity for joy that many Natives have, without having to give up the benefits of modern civilization. But no one has yet figured out how to combine the better aspects of the two cultures, the old and the new, without including the headaches. And Congress has now by law given the people of Alaska a goodly share of the headaches.

Congress has also been profligate when it comes to the disposition of the Alaskan land under both the Statehood Act and ANCSA. Largely ignoring its integrity, both of these Acts have resulted in the treatment of the Alaska land something like a giant pie to be sliced up into small pieces and passed to everyone who has his hand out. Along with compounding the fragmented ownership of the land, the framers of ANCSA seem, too, to have forgotten the hard lessons learned from the railroad grants of the mid-nineteenth century, for the Act not only makes possible, but sometimes obligatory, the checkerboard pattern of land ownerships that has long plagued land planners and administrators. Furthermore, the division of Alaska into corporate ownerships that must pay out their stock to thousands of shareholders in 1991 will almost inevitably cut up the land into numerous and relatively small pieces of private property, an idea that would have been anathema to earlier people here. The more than 240 recognized Village Corporations, scattered all over the state, have now begun parceling out lots within their boundaries. The state, which is demanding second crack at choosing Alaska's territory, is stepping up its selections. A map of Alaska showing land ownerships present and proposed already looks like a complex jigsaw puzzle; and this is of course only the beginning.

There is one ray of hope. ANCSA provides for sizable withdrawals of federal land reserves. And despite the arguments of the state, it is generally interpreted that the Act gives second priority, following the Village selections, to these federal selections. According to the ANCSA terms, the Secretary of the Interior is entitled to withdraw 45 million acres of land designated for multiple use management by the Bureau of Land Management. He is also entitled to set aside up to 80 million acres of lands to be considered for inclusion in the Four Systems, that is the National Park System, the National Wildlife System, the National Wild Rivers System and the National Forest System. His selection of these lands is subject to congressional review and approval. Secretary Rogers C. B. Morton has already made his selections, but conservationists believe that his choices have too often been misplaced and inadequate. The conservationists, in turn are proposing the withdrawal of national interest lands (within the framework of ANCSA) which they believe will more realistically gain the maximum protection and preservation of Alaska that is still possible. Congress will consider their proposals as well as those of the Administration. These national interest lands in fact offer a final chance for saving Alaska's great living resources, including some of the last great wild animal populations of the North American continent. Aware of this fact, some of the Native groups are supporting, at least informally, certain of the conservationists' national interest land proposals.

But inevitably there is serious conflict among the various parties concerned with this, the final major subdivision of Alaska. Despite all the vast reaches of territory, there simply isn't enough of the kind of land desired by everybody to go around, a fact that Congress evidently overlooked in writing ANCSA. Tentative Native and federal selections already overlap. Proposed state and federal selections conflict as well, and the state is suing the Department of the Interior to gain precedence in its land selection. Many Alaskans, too, whether they have lived in the state for twenty-five years or six months, bitterly resent the setting aside of *any* major federal reservations for protection of the land; they are calling the proposed national interest lands "just another federal land grab."

Yet the total acreage of national interest lands proposed by conservationists for protection in Alaska comes to about 107 million acres—little more than the 104 comparable million acres the state will get and much less than the state's eventual grand total of acreage. With a population of around 204 million American citizens, this averages out, in fact, to the equivalent of less than one half an acre per person. In contrast, by the terms of statehood, each Alaskan will be allotted the equivalent of about 410 acres of state land (based on a state population of 365,000). And on top of this, ANCSA, in its land grant of 40 million acres to some 75,000 Natives, will parcel out an average of an additional 550 acres to each one of these Alaskans.

While the conflict over the distribution of Alaskan acreage continues and selections are being made and revised, one area of Alaska has been committed irrevocably and clearly by the Native Claims Settlement Act; the 4.5 million-acre utility corridor from Prudhoe Bay to Valdez. This land withdrawal—an area considerably larger than the state of Connecticut—allows by no coincidence at all for the pipeline construction already laid out by the oil consortium (now known as Alyeska). A second 1-million-acre utility corridor, which skirts and isolates the magnificent Arctic Wildlife Range, has also been withdrawn, although not yet committed to use. The State of Alaska has not challenged these federal choices.

With the passage by Congress of legislation in 1973 approving construction of the pipeline—legislation that required the vote of then Vice President Spiro T. Agnew to break a tie in the Senate—the stage was set for construction of the largest and most costly construction project in the history of the free world. That which many people both inside and outside of Alaska had regarded with such deep apprehension became an inevitability. A pipeline will run from Prudhoe Bay, cross hundreds of miles of permafrost, breach the Brooks Range, and pass through some of the most unstable earthquake country on earth as it travels to Valdez. Economist George W. Rogers likens the structure to a potential "ecological Berlin Wall . . . dissecting the mainland mass of the state." It will imperil millions of acres of tundra and muskeg, as well as every river it crosses—including the mighty Yukon—with potential oil spills. Threatening the wildfowl of the Arctic Slope as well as the remaining major fishery resource of Prince William Sound, it promises an uncertain future for all of the wildlife whose territory it will traverse.

While the oil propagandists say that the building of this pipeline is like running "a string through your back yard," so vast is the territory through which it will pass, this analogy is specious. If the land is considered as a living organism, the construction of such a pipeline must inevitably be regarded as a major wound. And the laying open of the land is only the beginning. All the things that go with a massive construction effort—roads, heavy-equipment, facilities, graveled air strips, and so forth—not to mention the people and accelerated development that will inevitably follow—will compound the impact.

Indeed, with the construction of the pipeline now under way people have flocked to Alaska much as they did in the gold-rush days. The streets of Anchorage and Fairbanks are crowded with newly arrived cheechakos looking for jobs. Among them there exists the same fever of excitement, the same fervent expectations, and sometimes the same ruthlessness present three-quarters of a century ago. There will inevitably be the same bust when the oil is gone and the boom is over, but they do not talk about that.

But many long-time Alaskans do. There is growing unease, and even fear, of what is happening and of what lies ahead as the mightly pipeline construction moves along. The surplus of new jobseekers is swelling the already too-large ranks of unemployed. Housing facilities are badly overstrained and becoming more so. There is more vandalism of property and of the land. Public health problems are increasing. And there are no ready answers to today's problems, let alone tomorrow's.

Meantime, to allay the loudly voiced concerns of environmentalists everywhere, the oil companies, the state, and the federal government continue to assure the world that the pipeline will not destroy the "ecology" of the terrain through which it will pass. State and federal regulations have been drawn up and elaborate plans for protective devices are being developed to "guarantee" against oil spills. "House" ecologists of different oil companies roam the North Slope, plant exotic grass seed in the wounded tundra, plan for bridges and tunnels to "insure" the passage of the migrating caribou, and bemoan the too-often accurate potshots which have been taken by local personnel at the wildlife—the fox, wolf, wolverine, caribou, and even the bear. The monitoring of the construction of the pipeline will pose a major challenge; Congress in its wisdom has made it illegal for a suit to be brought to halt construction of the project and has waived further Environmental Impact Statement requirements as well. The hard fact emerges that, despite the good words and good intentions, no one can say how profound the damage will be.

And so as the tides of migratory birds mark the circling of the seasons, as the long summers invigorate the Alaskan land, and the winters lock it in their icy grip, the most crucial chapter of Alaskan history is being written. For the people who live there, it is an immediate and personal matter. In very human fashion, each Alaskan thinks of the land as belonging to him. It is easy for the Natives to claim prior ownership; Alaska was the home of their ancestors. It is easy for other Alaskans to think of their great state as a sovereign domain (and many wish it could be, if they wouldn't have to foot the bills). It is natural enough to resent the "outsiders," who would delay land selections, insist on better planning, urge long-term considerations as opposed to short-term economic gain, and work for large federal withdrawals for the protection of the land and its life. Standing on the boardwalk of a native village and viewing the immense stretches of tundra rolling softly into the horizon, it seems as though the world "outside" is unreal, and only a dream. Even walking along the streets of Anchorage and watching the light change on the snowy mountains which encircle the place, it is sometimes hard to remember that Alaska is the forty-ninth state of the Union and that legally its public lands belong to all Americans—to the people of Los Angeles and New York as much as to those who live in this city and in Juneau, Fairbanks, and Point Barrow. For those outsiders who have not seen Alaska, it is equally hard to realize how much, how incalculably much, is now at stake in this beautiful and vigorous yet fragile land.

Here is one of earth's last great relatively unspoiled wildernesses. Although we call it ours, in reality, it belongs to no person or persons, as earlier Americans seemed to know far better than we. It is an integral part of the biosphere, home for life that has taken eons to build itself into successful balance, life that is tied inextricably into the web of living things which enmeshes the planet. Earth's web of life is presently being weakened everywhere by the activities of people; its threads are being torn loose, unraveled, and destroyed. The delicate living environments of the Arctic and sub-Arctic regions—and the lives of countless creatures—are now under particular human pressure, in Siberia and Canada as well as in Alaska, as the quest is stepped up for earth's limited supply of minerals. It happens that the decisions about Alaska rest in our hands: this great land is our special trust at this crucial time.

Much of Alaska is now committed, and we will have to make the most of the decisions that we and others have already made. But there are still areas where we have a choice. In the national interest lands we have a last chance—our only remaining vehicle for preserving a sizable portion of Alaska and its life. What we decide to do with these lands will make the difference.

We can consider them as did the people who knew them long before we did—as a priceless heritage to be treasured and passed on intact. Or we can yield to the inevitably increasing pressures to exploit these vulnerable places too, and so follow in the footsteps of the earlier despoilers of the American West. A case can be made that those men were ignorant of what they were doing and that there were indeed new places for them to move on to, new fields to be cleared and plowed, new forests to be cut. No such case can be made for us. For we know that the Arctic land is easily destroyed. We know, too, and incontrovertibly, that all life on the planet is tied together and that our land and air and water, all our resources, are indeed finite. What we decide to do now in Alaska will be a measure of our wisdom. It will be a measure of our love for other living things with which we share our planet home. And ultimately, it will be a measure of our concern for the survival not just of ourselves, but of our children—and theirs.

Epilogue

The National Heritage: Looking to the Future

EDGAR WAYBURN

Part of the philosophy the first white settlers brought to the New World was the conviction that the land and its resources were meant to be owned and exploited by human beings. This land ethic, rooted deep in Judeo-Christian beliefs, had already profoundly changed the face of Europe. It was to have an equally profound effect on the virgin territory of North America. It resulted in the dispossession of the native peoples and the extinction of their cultures. It brought about the destruction of wildlife and the taming of the wilderness. It caused the clearing of the land in order to prepare it for the plow. In many places, it caused men to mine the land for its treasures. It occasioned the introduction of new and more tractable species of animals and plants. As time went on and the age of technology dawned, it finally resulted in radical rearrangement of the terrain, in the creation of huge new lakes, the rerouting of rivers, the encasement of the soil in vast areas of concrete.

From the beginning, this land ethic entailed the concepts of public and private lands, concepts reflected in a body of laws intended to facilitate the disposition, development, and exploitation of these lands. (Only within the past century did laws begin to reflect a concern for preserving the land.) The public lands were divided into states of the Union, and into pieces of private property, pieces that grew progressively smaller as the population grew progressively larger. Eventually, there was no more new land to appropriate and our resources proved to be limited. But the desire for new land and more resources did not abate. And so we are turning now to Alaska.

As we move into this, our last virgin territory, we are taking with us once again the land ethic and the land laws of our forefathers. But we are finding Alaska to be a very different land from the ones our forefathers settled. Alaska is at once a beautiful yet forbidding place. It is also very delicate and slow to heal. In many areas the climate is harsh and demanding. The mountains are enormous, and the glaciers the greatest in North America. Alaska is a land on a huge scale, where there have developed very special ecosystems which require both great space and freedom (qualities with which too many of us are unacquainted).

We have discovered already that many of our land laws are obsolete here. How can one "clear" a 160-acre homestead in the tundra, or subdivide a moving glacier into lots? As we go about exploiting Alaska, we are finding that many of our usual land-use practices are also unworkable. For example, one cannot farm in a region of permafrost, no matter how hard one tries. As Frank Fraser Darling put it, "Biologically, Alaska is wildlife country . . . [and] too many . . . conceive development along lines familiar in the kinder lands of the United States." It is becoming more and more obvious that Alaska cannot survive the methods of land use we have practiced in the lower 48 states.

Alaska's survival should concern all of us; fortunately, it does concern many of the people who are now making decisions about its future. For example, many of the Native Alaskans, who have had a long, close association with the land and its living resources, want to preserve both. Though the state government wants to make the most of the economic opportunities that this land offers, many Alaskans themselves do not want to see the country, the wildlife and the wilderness—the very things that pulled them northward—destroyed. The state and federal governments, working together in a joint Federal-State Land Use Planning Commission will make recommendations about the future disposition of Alaskan lands, decisions that we hope will reflect the desire of Alaskans to preserve their land.

Most of the people concerned with the survival of Alaska agree that the best way to save it and its unique assets is to preserve and maintain as much as possible the integrity of its land and life. At present there is still a great opportunity to set aside large parcels of public land. These lands must embrace, insofar as possible, all the important ecosystems of Alaska, such as those of the Arctic and subarctic, those of the migratory bird flyways, and those of the wild animal ranges. They must include the state's magnificent scenic areas and the superb geological features. They must preserve the rare archeological resources of the western shores. And the land must be selected with an understanding that these areas are not merely of local, but of national concern; they are as valuable to all the people of the United States as are the oil reserves of the North Slope.

Inevitably the question arises: how many acres should be set aside? How much is enough? Ideally, scientific land-use studies would give us an accurate estimate of the carrying capacity of the different areas involved—that is, the capability of the land to sustain its present biota, allowing for the incursions of man. But by law we have not allowed ourselves the time for such necessary studies: the Alaskan Native Claims Settlement Act requires the final determination of overall land ownership in the state by 1978. What evidence conservationists have indicates we should set aside at least 106 million acres if we are to preserve Alaska's important wildlife and scenic assets. In general, this is the approximate acreage identified by the Department of the Interior as being of special value (identified as reserved land, or as being of ecological concern). The Secretary of the Interior, however, has set aside considerably less land than this, not all of which has been selected primarily for protection. Of the approximately 83 million acres he has designated for consideration by Congress, over 18 million acres would be managed by the U. S. Forest Service, which, employing its multiple-use policy, would afford too little protection for those lands. Another 10 million acres are nominally listed as wildlife refuge lands but would be managed primarily for multiple use by the Bureau of Land Management.

Conservationists believe it is surely wiser to choose the larger figure, to preserve as much land as possible in our time and leave future generations the option of changing our decision. They therefore support strongly two bills (*S2918, Jackson* and *HR13564, Udall*) introduced into the 93rd Congress to gain maximum protection for Alaska. (Details of these bills are described below.)

In a society that has traditionally encouraged exploitation and subdivision of its land, setting aside the large acreages that need protection will not be easy. Our present land laws are inadequate to protect what is left of the unreserved Public Domain: it remains for Congress to enact new ones. Since no single governmental agency is equipped to handle the acquisition and maintenance of all the lands to be set aside, it is necessary to turn to three systems within the Department of the Interior: the National Park System, the National Wildlife Refuge System, and the National Wild and Scenic Rivers System. Each of the managing agencies is equipped to do a part of the job. Cooperatively, they may achieve the best possible protection for the Alaskan land and its life.

Along with the philosophical and mechanical problems of setting aside large parcels of federal land in Alaska, the withdrawals also face opposition from the enormously strong economic interests already at work in the state. In a world of increasing mineral shortages, it is easy to argue that every inch of the Alaskan land must be explored for its mineral potential. In a world hungry for wood, it is easy to urge the harvest of every tree. While those of us who live in lots 50 by 100 feet may find mind-boggling the prospect of establishing reserves in Alaska totaling 106 million acres, it is perhaps time to pause and consider certain hard realities. Our American land, our entire planet for that matter, is showing signs of stress from human use. Our air and our waters contain poisons. Our topsoil is wearing thin. The land ethics conceived 2,000 years ago in simpler nontechnological societies may be wearing thin as well. Our lives, like those of all living things, depend upon a healthy, well-functioning biosphere. Let us recall these things as we turn toward Alaska, where we still have a choice—and a chance.

As long as a boundary is only a line on a map, it does not interfere with wild creatures. One caribou herd, for instance, presently migrates regularly from Canada, across the international border, through the Arctic Wildlife Range, across the pipeline utility corridor, through lands that will be selected by Alaskan natives, down through lands still unclassified by the United States government, and back again. The caribou are unaware throughout that the terrain they use, and require, is, in fact, under different jurisdictions and ownerships. But when boundaries are transferred from paper to the land itself, when fences are erected or roads built or pipelines constructed, the wild animals will be forced to change their patterns. They will certainly avoid the many people who are inevitably drawn into a region during and after such construction, and the disruption of ancient behavior patterns may have unfortunate consequences for the health of the herd.

With these facts in mind, conservationists are proposing national interest reservations to guarantee the preservation of a maximum range for the last of America's free-roaming wild animals, and for one of the world's largest bird populations. Without such protection, these wild creatures are as doomed as were many of those once plentiful in the lower 48 states a century ago.

Other values also are given consideration in the recommendations for areas to be protected as national interest reservations. Alaska's plant communities, as unique as its wildlife populations, are necessary to the survival of all its life. Evolved through the millenia, they, too, require careful treatment if they are to be preserved. Of course, both Alaska's plants and its animals offer important opportunities for scientific study. So, too, does the rich trove of archeological sites in Alaska, most of which have not yet been explored. They may yield clues to man's earliest arrival in North America.

Alaska's scenery, as Henry Gannett pointed out decades ago, is perhaps her greatest asset, economically as well as esthetically—so long as it is not destroyed. The proposed national interest reservations offer the best possible chance to preserve most of these values.

But perhaps the most important values that the national interest reservations will protect are human values. With maximum land protection, the Alaskan Natives' human habitat will be best preserved and their cultures best kept alive. More broadly, all the people of the United States will benefit. Alaska's scenic treasures obviously offer extraordinary experiences for tourists and outdoor enthusiasts, be they hikers, fishermen, hunters, mountain climbers, birdwatchers, canoeists, or kayakers. More profoundly, Alaska's pure wilderness—her unspoiled beauty, vast open spaces, and sense of freedom provide refreshment and inspiration to the human spirit. Unlike Alaska's economic resources, this intangible "commodity" is difficult to measure. But, in a world of increasing pressures, it is perhaps more valuable. Like oil, pure wilderness is becoming increasingly scarce. Like oil, once it is consumed, it is gone forever. In Alaska we have our last and finest supply.

At this moment in American history, Alaska is unquestionably our most important national land asset. We must treat it that way, recognizing, at the same time, that it is of international significance as well. Several of the areas proposed in the national interest reservations directly involve other nations as, for instance, Canada in both the Arctic Wildlife Range and the international park proposed in the Wrangell, Chugach, and St. Elias Mountains. Every continent on earth is tied to Alaska. We know, for example, that birds from all over the world depend upon Alaska's wetlands for their survival. In ways less obvious and less understood, all of Alaska is an important part of the ecosphere. It is in our own enlightened self-interest to maintain as much as possible the integrity of this great land. Hence these proposals for seven areas to be set aside as national interest reservations.*

AREA A
The Arctic and Subarctic Lands and Life

In this superbly scenic region north of the Arctic Circle stands the Brooks Range, its summits rising to over 9,000 feet and forming some of the continent's most beautiful peaks. Even farther north, the rolling foothills of this range meet the immense, flat sweep of the Arctic Slope, which tilts beneath the Arctic Ocean. To the west, the mountains subside, and the Noatak River drainage carries their water southwest into the Bering Sea. Southward, clear streams flow into the Yukon and Kobuk river systems. On the east, this area is demarcated by the utility corridor through which the trans-Alaska pipeline passes.

*NOTE: *See pages 110 and 111 for a map of the National Interest Lands proposed for protection by conservationists. The map indicates the locations of all seven national interest areas.*

This Arctic and subarctic area contains a rich variety of flora, including prime examples of the four major tundra communities and boreal forest, or taiga communities. Although under pressure, and in some instances endangered by hunting, the region's wildlife is still plentiful, still able to roam freely. The animals include grizzly bear, wolf, wolverine, and fox, as well as North America's largest caribou herd, the Arctic herd. Containing some of the continent's prime migratory wildfowl habitat, the area is used by numerous and diverse nesting and resting migrants, and by such year-round residents as the snowy owl and the endangered, gyrfalcon and peregrine falcon.

The proposed national interest reservations in this region would not only protect important and fragile interrelated ecosystems but would also provide some of Alaska's most readily enjoyed wilderness. In the summer the area offers unequalled opportunities to backpackers, fishermen, naturalists, rock-climbers, and boaters. Bolder adventurers, like Robert Marshall, who named the two spectacular peaks guarding the headwaters of the North Fork of the Koyukuk River the "Gates of the Arctic," can enjoy this country in other seasons as well.

The total area of the four units proposed for the Arctic and subarctic national interest lands is 24 million acres, approximately the same acreage as that of the United States Navy's Petroleum Reserve No. 4, which was set aside for oil exploration.

Unit A-1
THE GATES OF THE ARCTIC NATIONAL PARK

Spanning the central section of the Brooks Range is the proposed 12.2-million-acre Gates of the Arctic National Park proposal.

The area is of great geological and biological importance, containing beautifully folded and arched rocks formed from Paleozoic sediments, as well as younger, more precipitous granite peaks. It includes the Killik watershed, the only Arctic Slope river system available for protection within a park. The tundra and the boreal forest communities are also represented in bountiful proportions.

An abundance of wildlife is found here, including the Arctic caribou herd, many grizzly bear, Dall sheep, moose, wolves, various raptors, and such fish as trout, pike, and char. Essentially, the region's wildlife communities are still complete, the food chain still intact. This park would give the highest

degree of protection to the passes used as migration routes by part of the Arctic herd's 240,000 animals.

The wild rivers within this proposed park include the swift and challenging upper Kobuk, flowing out of Walker Lake, and the more gentle Alatna, below Arrigetch Creek, both of which offer excellent recreational opportunities.

A proposal similar to the Gates of the Arctic National Park has been offered by the Arctic Slope Native Corporation. Entitled the Nūnamiut (People of the Land) National Park, this proposal differs in certain significant ways. It would include most of the lands proposed for the Gates of the Arctic park, plus lands from the proposed Noatak National Ecological Reserve, and lands presently allotted to the Arctic Slope Corporation for selection. Furthermore, it would classify certain lands to be used for Native subsistence and/or residency as the Nūnamiut Wildlands. It would establish in addition two wilderness areas. It would involve deeply the Natives in the decision to establish a national park contiguous to their homeland, as well as in the operation of future park facilities.

Several provisions of the proposed Nūnamiut National Park, however, are exclusionary, and inconsistent with national park objectives. Special rights within park boundaries are accorded the Natives, which should, in fairness, be extended to all the nation's people. Yet to extend these rights to all would endanger the land. The Nūnamiut proposal also gives special rights to the resident Natives to explore for and exploit possible oil and gas reserves within the park, a provision obviously inconsistent with national park criteria.

Nonetheless, joint cooperation between the Natives of the Arctic Slope Corporation, the National Park Service, and conservationists is highly desirable to achieve protection of this magnificent Arctic land. Such cooperation could result in the preservation of the major part of its extraordinary assets.

Unit A-2
THE NOATAK NATIONAL ECOLOGICAL RESERVE

West of the Gates of the Arctic region the Arctic caribou herd wanders through the 7.8 million acres proposed for the Noatak Ecological Reserve. Grizzly bear, Dall sheep, moose, wolves, and numerous species of birds also inhabit this beautiful and geographically varied expanse. The Eskimo Curlew, nearly extinct, is supposed to survive here. In the Noatak drainage large valleys are cut by two principal river systems. The Noatak, with its headwaters in the glaciers of spectacular Mt. Igikpak, flows through narrow canyons and broad plateaus, forming in one area the mountain-edged "Grand Canyon of the Noatak." The Squirrel River, one of the loveliest rivers draining the Brooks Range, is the major tributary of the Kobuk. Along with these two major river systems, both of which offer superb float opportunities, there are 650 miles of significant tributary waters, a dozen large lakes, and three mountain ranges studded with gemlike lakes and laced with streams.

This region provides particularly fine examples of forest and tundra ecotone, which is an area of overlap between two separate ecosystems. There is vast opportunity here for significant research, as well as for recreation. The area is now only minimally affected by civilization; the watershed of the Noatak has been largely unaffected by man, except for the activities of one small Native village, which have been minimal. The Natives presently depend upon subsistence hunting and fishing for their food, and overall protection of the resources is vital for their needs. This is one of the fragile areas which may present potential conflict with the desires of the outside recreationist.

This wilderness area would connect the proposed Gates of the Arctic National Park to the proposed Kobuk Valley National Monument and the proposed Selawik National Wildlife Range. Together, these four units, in combination with the costal areas discussed later, would preserve a remarkable expanse of beautiful Arctic and subarctic land and life.

Unit A-3
THE KOBUK VALLEY NATIONAL MONUMENT

The proposed Kobuk Valley National Monument contains 1.9 million acres of easily accessible and friendly terrain. Located in northwestern Alaska, this region's green tundra-swathed hills offer pleasant scenery and exceptional recreational opportunities, including camping, hiking, and river running.

The Arctic caribou herd roams throughout this area in migration and in the winter along with moose, wolves, black bear, and grizzly bear. The boreal forest here reaches its northwestern bounds. Archeological sites are of major importance within the proposed monument. (At the adjacent Onion Portage, there is an unusually rich site, with over 30 successive cultures represented.) With Native cooperation, much can be done to tell the story of man's use of this hospitable area in the deep past.

Of equal importance in this area are the unique Great and Little Kobuk Sand Dunes, which cover 25 square miles, the surviving traces of what once was a 300-square-mile expanse of inland dunes. These dunes are extremely important to the surrounding ecosystems that have evolved around them. They provide a dramatic contrast to the surrounding mountains, tundra, wetlands, and flood-plain forests. Within this undamaged dune area, scientists have a valuable laboratory for studying plant succession.

The lower Kobuk River is easily travelled by river-boat, and the Salmon is a delightful float stream.

Unit A-4
THE SELAWIK NATIONAL WILDLIFE RANGE

The establishment of the Selawik National Wildlife Range on the south of the Kobuk National Monument would add 2.1 million acres to the national wildlife refuge system. This area is of vital importance because of its extremely high population of nesting and breeding waterfowl. Its duck population alone exceeds 40 birds to the square mile, with nearly 350,000 of these waterfowl participating in the autumn flight. It serves, too, as an essential resting place for birds migrating between Asia and North America. The proposed Selawik Range also shelters the endangered gyrfalcon and peregrine falcon, and has a large mammal population as well. It is essential to the maintenance of that portion of the Arctic caribou herd that makes this area its wintering range.

AREA B
The Arctic-Interior Ecosystem

The 4.5-million-acre utility corridor for the trans–Alaska pipeline cuts through the Brooks Range and forms a boundary between the proposed Gates of the Arctic National Park and the terrain to the east. The national interest reservations proposed in Area B begin east of the pipeline and extend north-south in an attempt to maintain the essential integrity of the Arctic and subarctic ecosystems, from the northern coast south into the interior. This area includes in its southern part a portion of the intermontane plateau (an extension of the basin and range province) and to the north a segment of the Arctic Slope (an extension of the Great Plains). It contains Arctic peaks and inland wetlands comprised of more than 25,000 miles of streams, at least 40,000 lakes and ponds, and parts of two major rivers (the historic Yukon and the Porcupine), as well as the Charley River Basin.

This extensive and varied area is tied together by its wildlife, which roams freely throughout the units. Its integrity is essential to two major caribou herds. It is possible that the ranges of these animals that extend into Canada can be protected by a cooperative agreement with the Canadian government. The area also contains some of America's most important migratory bird habitats.

Within the area is a geological wonderland, an unbroken record that extends back at least a half-million years. Paleontologists can study ice-age mammals preserved in its frozen soil. The uplands included in the interior portions have been likened to the Adirondacks and are delightful for hiking and camping. The various rivers are ideal for float recreation. Though bitterly cold in winter, this region is warm, dry, and sunny throughout the summer months, generally providing highly enjoyable weather for travelers and outdoorsmen.

Unit B-1

THE ARCTIC NATIONAL WILDLIFE RANGE

The 9-million-acre Arctic National Wildlife Range was established in 1960 to preserve unique wildlife and wilderness. More than 200 miles of valleys along its western and southern edges, however, were excluded from the range, and these lands are essential to maintaining the free-roaming animal populations the range was established to protect. The range should be enlarged to the west and south by the addition of 5.6 million acres. Within the proposed additions are two superb rivers, the south-flowing Wind and the north-flowing Ivishak, both good float streams.

The fragile terrain and pure wilderness of this Arctic region provide a home for such animals as the musk ox, wolverine, and grizzly bear, as well as for moose, wolf, Dall sheep, and red fox. Its bird life includes two varieties of the endangered peregrine

falcon. Two herds of caribou depend upon both the range and the area proposed for addition: the Porcupine herd of 150,000 animals calve in the existing range after migrating through the proposed southern extension. Part of the larger Arctic caribou herd migrates through the proposed western extension.

It is essential that the withdrawal for a million-acre utility corridor for oil and gas pipelines now within this area be revoked.

Unit B-2

THE YUKON FLATS NATIONAL WILDLIFE RANGE

The proposed Yukon Flats National Wildlife Range, lying immediately south of the Arctic National Wildlife Range, would comprise 12.3 million acres. Here, tens of thousands of lakes, tarns, and ponds, more than 25,000 miles of streams, and uncounted acres of wet spruce bog, or muskeg, make this one of the single most productive waterfowl habitats on earth. More than 2 million ducks are supported in this vast river basin, which includes the confluence of the Porcupine and Yukon rivers. Between 10 and 15 percent of the canvasbacks in North America are born here.

Besides its importance to the survival of at least 20 species of waterfowl that nest here, the Yukon Flats region is vital to certain rare or endangered species, including the peregrine falcon. The upland regions of the Yukon Flats also provide a good habitat for Dall sheep. Salmon fill the rivers and play an essential role in the life of the Athabascan Indians, whose homeland this region is.

Although this part of the interior lies still and frozen during the long, dark, frigid months of winter, it pulses furiously with an abundance of life during the hot summer days. This area is essential for the lasting protection of literally millions of living creatures.

Unit B-3

YUKON-CHARLEY RIVERS NATIONAL PARK

The Yukon River is Alaska's most important waterway. Historically, it has been a thoroughfare for explorers, traders, miners, boatmen, tourists, and recreationists, not to mention salmon. Biologically, it supports an enormous percentage of Alaska's wildlife, including, in the flats and delta, over three-fourths of the state's migratory waterfowl. This river is the dominant element in maintaining and supporting the 150 to 200 species of birds that use the sloughs and ponds along its course. Its periodic flooding enriches the adjacent lands, and renews the delicate ecosystems along its banks.

No part of the Yukon River is now protected within park boundaries. The proposed 2-million acre Yukon-Charley Rivers National Park would take in a historic stretch of the upper Yukon, a section that runs through mountainous terrain. Important concentrations of the peregrine falcon and other raptors occur here. The park would embrace rangelands required by thousands of caribou for their calving and wintering grounds and would also protect such distinctive species as the lynx and wolverine, as well as grizzly bear, wolf, and fox.

The wonderfully clear Charley River is an excellent float stream that winds between cliffs where Dall sheep wander. Its upland region provides extremely pleasant hiking ground. Upstream, tundra and spruce forests interweave in intricate complexity. This pristine watershed, little changed by either glaciation or people, is a particularly significant park proposal in that it supports flora and fauna of nearly every major Alaskan interior species, including such bird rarities as nesting surf birds, Smith's longspurs and grayheaded or Siberian chickadees.

AREA C
South Central-Southeast Alaska

Unit C-1
THE WRANGELL-KLUANE INTERNATIONAL PARK

This proposed International Park has perhaps the most exciting potential of any of the national interest lands. Stretching north beyond the Wrangells across the Alaska range and into the upper Tanana Valley, southeast to Glacier Bay National Monument, and due south to the Gulf of Alaska, its proposed 18.1 million acres in Alaska encompass some of the most spectacular alpine scenery to be found anywhere on earth. Certain portions of the mountain ranges in this area sweep into Canada and are now protected in Canada's 6.8-million-acre Kluane National Park and Game Sanctuary. Canadian park officials have expressed interest in joining an even larger area to the American park to form what could be earth's single greatest natural scenic reserve.

The area offers a remarkable assortment of scenic and geological features. The narrow, recently uplifted coastal region reaches a height of 18,008 feet at Mt. St. Elias (and over 19,200 feet at Mt. Logan, in nearby Canada). At the feet of these immense snow-covered pinnacles stretch heavily forested, rain-drenched lowlands. The ice and snow fields of the coastal mountains feed both the single largest glacier on the continent, the Malaspina, and the longest, the Bering. These mountains contain the most extensive glacial system in the United States, and the greatest concentration of peaks over 14,500 feet in North America.

However, the Wrangell-Kluane Park proposal has much more than mountains. There are some of the continent's loveliest lakes, such as Copper, Rock and the three Tebays. There are spectacular ice-sculptured valleys, rolling foothills, and the beautiful coastal plain. The lowlands offer precious hospitable country for the hiker, backpacker, or camper. This living space, presently threatened by mining operations, and possibly by logging, is essential to the integrity of the total area, as well as to its wildlife. The wildlife resources of the region include the endangered glacier bear, and many other Alaskan mammals. Many songbirds, and even hummingbirds, nest in this region. Its numerous streams offer prodigious sport fishing, and its larger rivers, all kinds of floating experiences. The Alsek River, rising in Canada, is fringed and fed by numerous glaciers, and its full length has been run successfully only once. It attracts none but the most daring and expert kayakers or those willing to make an arduous portage across a glacier. The Copper River, on the other hand, offers superb, safe stretches for canoeing.

This area is the target of numerous special interests. Its mineral resources, still not fully determined, but apparently very localized, are considered highly significant by some geologists, although their economic exploitation is presently questionable. There are also demands on the forested areas for logging.

The Ahtna Native Regional Corporation, whose lands are adjacent to the proposed Wrangell-Kluane International Park, is interested in the proposed park and has indicated its support. They wish to be, and should be involved in the planning of the park and, later, in its administration.

Unit C-2
NATIONAL FOREST ADDITIONS

Two areas located in south-central and southeast coastal Alaska are proposed as additions to the national forest system, which is administered by the Secretary of Agriculture. The proposed lands are logical additions of 900,000 acres to the existing 16-million-acre Tongass National Forest, and 700,000 acres to the existing 5-million-acre Chugach National Forest. These boundary expansions are designed to incorporate contiguous lands suitable to national forest objectives under a single management authority.

Unit C-3
THE KENAI FJORDS NATIONAL MONUMENT

Due south of Anchorage at a distance of about 120 miles, or two and a half hours of traveling time, is the proposed Kenai Fjords National Monument. Its 300,000 acres extend from the top of the Harding Ice Field along land recently exposed by retreating glaciers, past a deeply dissected coast, and three miles out to sea. The resulting unobstructed ice field-fjord ecological system is unique. The ice field itself, one of only a few in the United States, is unusually accessible, and also contains numerous scenic, and scientific, and wildlife values.

Many glaciers rise from the Harding Ice Field, some carving their way to the "drowned" coast, some ending in blue-green lakes. The rugged coast is populated by a large variety of creatures. A visitor to one of the easily reached fjords has abundant opportunity to observe seals, sea lions, sea otters, whales, bear, moose, or bald eagles.

The Kenai fjords offer some of Alaska's best examples of the tide- and wave-churned lagoons and estuaries that support the giant Alaskan shrimp and king crab. These inlets sharply incise the land, and cliffs rise thousands of feet within scarcely a mile of the coast. Lush green forests of Sitka spruce, mountain hemlock, and western hemlock, along with soft grasslands, cover the region.

AREA D
The Alaska Range-Aleutian Chain

The Alaska Range and Aleutian Chain together form the northern ridge of Alaska's Pacific mountain system, one of North America's major physiographic features. This immense series of uplifts of the earth's crust terminates in the western edge of the continent. Within it, the continental land mass is upthrust to its highest point at Mt. McKinley and, below the sea, downwarped to its lowest point in the Aleutian Trench. A chain of glistening craters, many active, form a 1,700-mile chain, one arc in the Pacific Ocean's "Ring of Fire." Vulcanism, past as well as present, can be seen in unusual and varied geological displays.

While not all contiguous, the major units in the Alaska Range-Aleutian Chain area share many unique geological features, a rich and varied flora, some of earth's grandest scenery, and a waning, though still prodigious and diverse wildlife. Much of this country is easily explored on foot and provides for fine hiking and camping. Some of the world's finest sport fishing can be found in these regions of Alaska.

The boundaries of each proposed unit have been drawn to respect its particular ecosystem and/or wildlife range and to protect important watershed areas. Natural landmarks have been chosen to serve as boundary lines whenever possible.

Unit D-1
MT. MCKINLEY NATIONAL PARK

Mt. McKinley (named by the native peoples, *Denali, The Great One*) is not only North America's highest, but perhaps its single most magnificent mountain. It is also home for a spectacular array of wildlife. Mt. McKinley Park is presently one of the few places where one can easily observe at close range, and with relative ease, some of the remaining great wild animals of North America.

Mt. McKinley National Park was established in 1917 to protect the scenery of the great mountain as well as its abundant wildlife. The present boundary lines do neither. Over half the mountain massif, as well as its most spectacular glaciers, lie southeast of the present park. The range of its wolves, moose, caribou, and grizzly bear is lopped off on both the north and west. Major additions are therefore needed in the south, north, and west if the wildlife and scenic grandeur of America's greatest mountain are to be maintained. It is proposed to enlarge Mt. McKinley National Park from 2 million to 6.2 million acres.

Unit D-2
LAKE CLARK NATIONAL PARK

The 5.8 million acres proposed for Lake Clark National Park rise from the coast of Cook Inlet on the east, straddle the massive Alaska and Aleutian mountain ranges, and extend to the rolling hills on the west. The area is marked by unusual topography and geological diversity from volcanoes and glaciers to spectacular coast. The region is bejeweled with blue lakes set in meadowlike tundra. The lakes are fed by and feed in turn many waterfalls and streams, which are vital for the spawning of the Bristol Bay salmon and rainbow trout. The variety of plants and wildlife is spectacularly representative of Alaska's natural abundance. Trumpeter swan, brown and black bear, wolves, bald eagles, and the Mulchatna caribou herd roam the region and will be offered substantial protection by the proposed park.

The network of valleys and river courses weaving their ways through the craggy mountains allow for relatively easy access to the inner reaches of the park. Because the Lake Clark area is only 100 miles west of Anchorage, wide use of this area can be expected.

Unit D-3
THE ILIAMNA NATIONAL WILDLIFE RANGE

At the heart of the proposed 1.6-million-acre Iliamna National Wildlife Range is Lake Iliamna, the seventh largest freshwater lake in the United States. While the region is noted for its significant geological and scenic values, the prime purpose of this range is to protect its wildlife, particularly the fish that spawn in its river systems. These rivers, including the beautiful Kvichak, are spawning waters for the world's largest remaining red salmon population. In addition, the streams support Alaska's finest trophy rainbow trout. Bristol Bay, into which the Kvichak flows, is considered one of the richest marine habitats on the continent.

The Beluga whale migrates to Lake Iliamna, and the only freshwater colony of seals in the United States lives here. Such threatened species as the osprey use the area for subsistence, and migrating birds use it heavily. In October, the entire world population of Emperor geese congregates in the Bristol Bay region. With the thousands of black brant also present at this time, they provide an unmatched experience for the fortunate viewer.

This is a prime area for recreationists and is already heavily used by fishermen and hunters from the nearby Anchorage metropolitan area. Human use must be controlled if the native wildlife is to survive. Many Native villages lie within the area and have the right of first selection of the land and waters. It is hoped that cooperative agreements can be arranged with them.

Unit D-4
KATMAI NATIONAL PARK

The 3-million-acre Katmai National Monument, which lies across the broad northeastern portion of the Alaska Peninsula, was established by presidential proclamation in 1918, six years after a massive and extraordinary eruption of Mt. Novarupta, a small crater near Mt. Katmai. This eruption rained down thick layers of volcanic ash, which created the Valley of Ten Thousand Smokes.

Uniquely scenic, this cool, foggy region is rich in historical and archeological sites. It is vital to the continued existence of the Alaskan brown bear and the osprey, two species increasingly threatened by the incursions of man. The streams and lakes of the Katmai region are also needed by the red salmon. Among these waters, the Alagnak River, fed by blue-green glacial lakes, is an excellent float stream.

It is proposed that the monument be redesignated a national park and enlarged by 2.6 million acres on the north, west, and south. This redrawing of boundaries would protect the habitat of Katmai's wildlife, as well as its unique floral resources, which include forest, shrubland, grassland, wetland, tundra, lakeshore, and coastal communities. The boundaries would also be drawn to natural topographical, as well as more visually definable, landmarks and would place entire watershed systems under park service management.

Units D-5 and D-6
ANIAKCHAK CALDERA NATIONAL MONUMENT
AND THE ALASKA PENINSULA NATIONAL
BROWN BEAR REFUGE

Midway down the Alaska Peninsula is the proposed Aniakchak Caldera National Monument, an area of 700,000 acres. This caldera of an extinct volcano has formed a complete and inclusive environment of unusual scientific and scenic interest. Old lava flows are found side by side with recent examples of volcanic activity in an extraordinary 30-square-mile crater. Ringing this snow- and ice-streaked bowl are dark ash fields, where new plant communities are struggling to establish themselves. Within it lies the deep turquoise waters of Surprise Lake, which is fed by carbonate-laden springs. The Aniakchak River spills from this lake through a color-streaked gash in the crater's rim known as "The Gates."

The green, tundra-covered flanks of Aniakchak crater form an important habitat that supports populations of Alaskan brown bear and moose. The coastal waters are rich with life: sea lions, sea otters, seals, and sea birds are clustered here. Salmon, trout, and many other species of fish abound in the Aniakchak River (a wild but floatable stream) and other waterways in the proposed monument.

Surrounding the proposed Aniakchak Caldera National Monument and forming an important extension of its ecosystem is the proposed 4.9-million acre Alaska Peninsula National Brown Bear Range. This range would provide habitat for the giant brown bear, whose range will be greatly reduced in the present Kodiak National Wildlife Refuge as Native village corporations make their land selections. The proposed range would guarantee the survival of one of America's greatest land mammals, a species that vies with the polar bear for the distinction of being the continent's largest carnivore. This huge animal (specimens eleven and one-half feet tall have been reported) must have space to survive. One brown bear requires 64,000 acres of range to support himself. Caribou, wolves, moose, marine animals, and other species are also found on the Alaska Peninsula, which is one of the most important terrestrial and marine wildlife regions in Alaska.

AREA E
Western and Central Alaska Migratory Bird Sanctuaries

This outward edge of the continent is often foggy or cloud-shrouded. Its summer weather may be cool or even raw. Winds sweep from the sea, and trees are unable to gain a toehold, although the land itself is gentle and covered with a green carpet of tundra or wet taiga. In this region are some of Alaska's richest and most varied concentrations of life. In the Togiak area alone there are hundreds of different species of

plants and animals. And in the Yukon delta, in places presently unprotected, there are nesting and resting grounds for millions of birds.

Unit E-1
THE TOGIAK NATIONAL WILDLIFE RANGE

The proposed 3-million-acre Togiak National Wildlife Range extends from the Wood River-Tikchik Lakes (an area of superb beauty already selected by the state) west to Kuskokwim Bay. This refuge comprises an ecosystem that rises from sea level to the summit of a 5,000-foot-high watershed, thus embracing a diversity of wildlife and fish resources.

The region serves as a crossroads for waterfowl and shorebirds migrating from winter ranges in the Pacific. It offers shelter for the endangered Arctic peregrine falcon and supports one of Alaska's most diverse mammalian fauna, including 32 species of land mammals. Its rivers provide spawning waters for an abundance of salmon, steelhead, and trout.

Within the proposed range are numerous low but scenic mountains, great sweeps of upland tundra, jewellike lakes, and two superb wild rivers, the Kanektok and the Togiak.

Because it connects the existing Cape Newenham National Wildlife Refuge and three replacement refuges, the Togiak Refuge has additional value as an essential link in a much larger protected area.

Unit E-2
THE YUKON DELTA NATIONAL WILDLIFE RANGE

The establishment of the 5.4-million-acre Yukon Delta Wildlife Range will help preserve the second most productive habitat on the continent for migratory and nesting waterfowl. Along with 2 million ducks, geese, and swans, countless shorebirds breed in this area. Many of America's emperor geese and cackling geese are born here. There is an annual flight of more than 3 million waterfowl. This coastline habitat is used by birds, including shorebirds and waterfowl, en route to or from the Soviet Union, Australia, Antarctica, and South America.

Included in this proposal is the Andreafsky River watershed, which stretches inland and upward to include the transition from lowland forest to tundra. Within this region, the rare and little-known bristle-thighed curlew nests. The Andreafsky is a beautiful free-flowing river.

A number of Native villages are located within the proposed refuge. Most of their occupants—who total some 16,000—are still bound closely to the land and are now highly dependent upon it and its resources for their subsistence and way of life. These Eskimos have sponsored a program known as Nunam Kitlusisti ("protector of the land"), which has as its goals the education of the people to the values of the land and its wildlife, and the cooperation of the people in decisions regarding broad land use. The cooperation of these Yupik Eskimos can be hoped for in the establishment and maintenance of this and earlier established ranges.

Unit E-3
THE KOYUKUK NATIONAL WILDLIFE RANGE

The 8.2-million-acre Koyukuk National Wildlife Range contains five units that lie generally along the Yukon River between the Yukon flats and the Yukon delta. The wetlands in these units are used by countless waterfowl with international ranges. Nearly 800,000 ducks and geese rest in the marsh areas of the Koyukuk River in the fall, and the trumpeter swan finds shelter here. The entire region serves as a nesting and breeding ground for many other kinds of birds, as well as for mammals and fish.

In the Koyukuk area there is also a variety of sensitive species of animals. The wolverine and lynx, the grizzly bear, the fur-bearing marten, and the Arctic grayling utilize areas of the undisturbed marsh, meadow, stream, and mountain that this range would provide.

Unit E-4
THE COASTAL NATIONAL WILDLIFE REFUGE

The proposed Coastal National Wildlife Refuge is a series of islets, islands, rocks, pinnacles, and cliffs distributed along 1,500 miles of Alaskan coast, from Cape Lisburne in the Chukchi Sea to the Bering Islands in the Gulf of Alaska. The proposed areas, collectively amounting to 500,000 acres, "are of diverse origin and topography, and in extending through 15 degrees of latitude encompass a variety of climatic zones," according to the Department of the Interior.

Refuge status will primarily provide much-needed protection of nationally and internationally sig-

nificant marine birds and waterfowl and for the preservation of the hauling grounds and rookeries of marine mammals. Supported in this terrain and in the surrounding land and waters are 16 species of whales (7 of which are endangered), 28 species of marine mammals, the nesting sites of 4 to 6 million seabirds, and several endangered species, including the peregrine falcon and the gyrfalcon.

Significant biological research has been initiated at Cape Thompson and should be carried to its completion if its full value is to be appreciated. This proposal would provide such an opportunity.

AREA F
Northwest Alaska: Lands of the Bering Sea Bridge

During the Ice Age, when much of earth's water was frozen and locked into glaciers, the level of the sea was several hundred feet lower than it is today. It is believed that during these periods the North American continent was linked to Eurasia by a land bridge across the Bering Sea. Across this gateway came many mammals that are now extinct, among them the saber-toothed tiger, the woolly mammoth, and the mastodon. Their remains lie frozen in the ground in many parts of Alaska, reminders of a time now gone. The Bering Sea bridge was very likely the doorway to North America for people as well. Just when man first crossed it is not known, but some archeologists believe it was more than 40,000 years ago—perhaps much more. Many of these first people stayed in Alaska and left their relics sealed beneath the ash and lava flows. Their descendants still live in the same regions that were first settled.

Therefore, northwest Alaska is an area rich in archeological resources that are only now beginning to be investigated. It also contains unusual geological features and fine examples of coastal tundra (and indeed the entire arctic tundra-marine environment), as well as other types of tundra. In this region the boreal forest reaches its northwest limits. Marine life and land life are surprisingly rich and varied in the cool, damp, foggy climate of this region.

Immediately east lie the Noatak and Selawik, units of Area A. With the two units of Area F, the proposed national interest reserves in Alaska come full circle.

Unit F-1

THE CHUKCHI-IMURUK
NATIONAL ECOLOGICAL RESERVE

Approximately four million acres are proposed for protection in the Chukchi-Imuruk National Ecological Reserve, located on the Seward Peninsula. In this vast expanse of tundra, rich in human history and abundant in clues to human migration from Eurasia, internationally important research opportunities exist. In the northern regions of the proposed reserve, there are remnants of ash explosions considered unique. These have buried, in almost total preservation, ancient ecosystems. (The ash-drowned craters of earlier volcanoes now cradle deep-water lakes.) Over the southern portion of the proposed preserve, lava flows have encased what once was a varied tundra world. Scientists will be able to study the timeless physical features and ecological processes for a graphic picture of the transitions of the area from the prehistoric to the present, as well as earlier stages of plant and animal succession.

The shoreline in the Chukchi region is a nearly continuous strip of prehistoric and more recent Eskimo sites. The rich archeological opportunities present here are most important to the U. S. and its neighbor, the Soviet Union, only 56 miles away.

Botanists and biologists also will find significant material for study in this prime exhibit of the Arctic tundra-marine interface. Here can be found an exceptional transect of tundra communities from the coastal tundra (sedge) upward to the moist tundra (tussock), and the dry tundra (heath).

This unique scientific area is also an important migratory bird habitat. Hundreds of thousands of waterfowl, song birds, sea birds, and shorebirds fly from this Alaskan peninsula to virtually every continent. One hundred and twelve species of birds feed and rest here; 87 species nest. The Chukchi region has one of Alaska's densest duck populations.

Unit F-2

THE CAPE KRUSENSTERN NATIONAL MONUMENT

The proposed Cape Krusenstern National Monument is a 350,000-acre area situated north of the Arctic Circle on the shores of the Bering Sea. A number of geological and archeological factors make this Arctic coastal region, like the Chukchi-Imuruk, important.

Cape Krusenstern is an ancient and stable promontory, whose unusual beach ridges offer unique research opportunities in the study of fluctuating sea levels and coastal currents. The area has great biological significance. The coastal plain will also provide information about the cultures of the ancestors of today's Eskimos and about their progression throughout Alaska. This historical area should be preserved by the nation to recognize and protect the heritage of the Eskimo people.

AREA G
Wild and Scenic Rivers

The Alaskan scenery is threaded by a variety of beautiful free-flowing rivers, of which 39 have been recommended for inclusion in the national wild and scenic rivers system. A number of these rivers are wholly within the boundaries of the proposed national interest reserves. Special status as wild rivers will provide even further protection of their wilderness characteristics. For those rivers not in national parks or wildlife refuges, designation as wild and scenic rivers will serve to protect the entire course of the river, and allow for its consistent land-use management.

Each proposed river has its own special value and beauty. The primitive character of the Alaskan environment is exhibited in all the proposed rivers, which illustrate the closeness and harmony with which the Alaskan watersheds and wildlife coexist. Flowing through canyon-bound walls or expansive valleys covered with forests or interesting geologic landscapes, these pristine waterways are the mainstay of the wildlife of the land and sea. Their protection is essential if they are to sustain the countless birds that feed, rest, and nest along their shores and in their deltas and wetlands.

The following rivers within units of the national park system and national wildlife refuge system are proposed as components of the national wild and scenic rivers system and would be administered as wild rivers within the unit in which they are located:

Alagnak (Katmai)
Alatna (Gates of the Arctic)
Alsek (Wrangells)
Andreafsky (Yukon Delta)
Aniakchak (Aniakchak Caldera)
Black, including all tributaries (Yukon Flats)
Beaver Creek (Yukon Flats)

Bremner (Wrangells)
Charley (Yukon-Charley)
Chitina (Wrangells)
Copper (Wrangells)
Ivishak (Arctic)
Kanektok (Togiak)
Killik, including Easter Creek (Gates of the Arctic)
Kobuk (Gates of the Arctic)
Kuzitrin (Chukchi-Imuruk)
Mulchatna, including Chilikadrotna (Lake Clark)
Noatak, including Cutler, Aniuk, Kugururok, and
    Kelly (Gates of the Arctic and Noatak)
North Fork Koyukuk, including Tinayguk (Gates of
    the Arctic)
Nowitna (Koyukuk)
Porcupine (Yukon Flats)
Salmon (Kobuk Valley)
Sheenjek (Arctic and Yukon Flats)
Squirrel (Noatak)
Togiak (Togiak)
Wind (Arctic)

The following rivers outside of proposed national reservations are also proposed as wild rivers:

Birch Creek
Holitna
Hoholitna
Melozitna
Mulchatna
Nelchina
Nowitna
Susitna
Tazlina
Unalakleet

Three additional rivers are proposed for scenic river status: Delta, Forty Mile, and Gulkana.

Land Use Planning

The proposed National Interest Lands Reservations Act has a number of provisions important for land-use planning in Alaska:

1) Certain areas within proposed national reservation land boundries are withdrawn for possible selection by Native village or regional corporations. Such lands within the national reservations that are not selected by Native corporations are automatically recommended to Congress as part of the reserved lands.

Lands outside of the national reservations withdrawn for possible Native selection but not selected by Native corporations are to be studied by the Department of the Interior for two years to determine their value as part of the national conservation systems.

2) Whenever public lands identified for selection by the state of Alaska are added to national reservations, the secretary will make available for state selection other public lands of approximately equal acreage.

3) All lands established as national parks, national wildlife refuges, national ecological reserves or national wild or scenic rivers are withdrawn from all forms of appropriation under the public-land laws, including the mining and mineral-leasing laws. In the case of the national forests, the secretary may issue permits for metalliferous mining and leases for minerals to meet critical national needs.

4) The secretary is empowered to designate zones where subsistence uses are permitted, consistent with maintaining the biological productivity of the area.

5) Hunting, trapping, and fishing are allowed within the boundaries of the national wildlife refuge system, the wild and scenic rivers system, and in National Ecological Reserves, when it is determined that the productivity of the native species will not be impaired. Certain zones where these uses are not allowed will also be designated. More-over, subsistence uses are allowed within the new units of the National Park System, as well as in the other systems.

6) All of the new units established are to be studied for their possible inclusion as units of the national wilderness preservation system, with recommendations to Congress within ten years after passage of the act.

Selected Readings

Berton, Pierre. *The Klondike Fever, The Life and Death of the Last Great Stampede.* New York: Alfred A. Knopf, 1958.

Bohn, David. *Glacier Bay, The Land and the Silence.* San Francisco: Sierra Club, 1967.

Brooks, Paul. *Pursuit of Wilderness.* Boston: Houghton Mifflin & Co., 1971.

Burroughs, John, *et. al. Harriman Alaska Expedition,* Volumes I and II. New York: Doubleday Page Co., 1904.

Chance, Norman A. *The Eskimo of North Alaska, Case Studies in Cultural Anthropology.* New York: Holt, Rinehart, and Winston, 1966.

Chrisler, Lois. *Arctic Wild.* New York: Harper and Brothers, 1958.

Cooley, Richard A. *Alaska: A Challenge in Conservation.* Madison, Wisconsin: University of Wisconsin Press, 1966.

Darling, F. Fraser *Pelican in the Wilderness.* New York: Random House, 1956.

Farb, Peter. *Man's Rise to Civilization as Shown by the Indians of North America from Primeval Times to the Coming of the Industrial State.* Pages 34–53, 133–152. New York: E. P. Dutton, 1968.

Fejes, Claire. *People of the Noatak.* New York: Alfred A. Knopf, 1966.

Ford, Corey. *Where the Sea Breaks Its Back.* Boston: Little, Brown and Co., 1966.

Griggs, Robert F. *The Valley of the Ten Thousand Smokes.* Washington, D.C.: National Geographic Society, 1922.

Hunt, Charles B. *Natural Regions of the United States and Canada.* Pages 615–650. San Francisco: W. H. Freeman and Co., 1973.

Leopold, A. Starker and Darling, F. Fraser *Wildlife in Alaska, An Ecological Reconnaissance,* Reprint. Westport, Connecticut: Greenwood Press, 1973.

London, Jack. The Call of the Wild. New York: New American Library, Signet, 1971.

Marshall, Robert. *Alaska Wilderness, Exploring the Central Brooks Range,* 2nd ed. Berkeley, California: University of California Press, 1970.

Marshall, Robert. *Arctic Village.* New York: Quinn and Boder Co., 1933.

Mayokok, Robert. *Eskimo Customs.* Nome, Alaska: Nome Nugget, 1965.

Milton, John P. *Nameless Valleys, Shining Mountains, The Record of an Expedition into the Vanishing Wilderness of Alaska's Central Brooks Range.* New York: Walker and Co., 1970.

Muir, John. *Travels in Alaska.* Reprint. New York: AMS Press, Inc., 1970.

Murie, Adolph. *Mammals of Mount McKinley National Park, Alaska.* San Francisco: Mount McKinley Natural History Association, 1962.

———— *A Naturalist in Alaska.* New York: Devin-Adair, 1961.

———— *The Wolves of Mount McKinley.* Washington, D.C.: Government Printing Office, 1944.

Murie, Margaret E. *Two in the Far North.* New York: Alfred A. Knopf, 1962.

Murie, Olaus J. *Journeys to the Far North.* Palo Alto, California: American West Publishing Company, 1973.

Olsen, Richard C. (ed.) *The Living Wilderness* (Special Alaska Issue), January 1972. Washington, D.C.: The Wilderness Society.

Pewe, Troy L. *Permafrost and Its Effect on Life in the North.* Corvallis, Oregon: Oregon State University Press, 1970.

Rogers, George W. *Alaska in Transition, The Southeast Region.* Baltimore: JohnsHopkins Press, 1960.

———— (ed.) *Change in Alaska. People, Petroleum, and Politics.* Seattle: University of Washington Press, 1970.

———— *The Future of Alaska, Economic Consequences of Statehood.* Baltimore: Johns Hopkins Press, 1962.

Schwatka, Frederick. *A Summer in Alaska.* St. Louis: J. W. Henry, 1893.

Service, Robert W. *The Spell of the Yukon and Other Verses.* New York: Dodd Mead, n.d.

Sheldon, Charles, *The Wilderness of the North Pacific Coast Islands.* New York: Charles Scribner's Sons, 1912.

Sherwood, Morgan B. *Alaska and Its History.* Seattle: University of Washington Press, 1967.

———— *Exploration of Alaska, 1865–1900.* New Haven, Connecticut: Yale University Press, 1965.

Wahrhaftig, Clyde. *Physiographic Divisions of Alaska,* Professional Paper #482. Washington, D.C.: Government Printing Office, 1965.

Waxell, Sven. *The Russian Expedition to America.* New York: Collier Books, 1962.

Wright, Billie. *Four Seasons North, A Journal of Life in the Alaska Wilderness.* New York: Harper and Row, 1973.

PERTINENT LEGISLATION

Public Law 92-203: *The Alaska Native Claims Act.* 92nd Congress (HR 10367).

Legislation supported by conservationists: 93rd Congress
13564 (Mr. Udall) 93rd Congress, 2nd session. March 18, 1974.
S 2918 (Mr. Jackson) 93rd Congress, 2nd session. January 30, 1974.

Legislation supported by the Nixon Administration: 93rd Congress
HR 12336 (Mr. Haley *et. al.*) 93rd Congress, 2nd session. January 30, 1974.
S 2917 (Mr. Jackson and Mr. Fannin) 93rd Congress, 2nd session. January 30, 1974